Exposure
& other microfictions & prose poems

HOLLY HOWITT &
JAN FORTUNE-WOOD (eds)

Published by Cinnamon Press
Meirion House
Glan yr afon
Tanygrisiau
Blaenau Ffestiniog
Gwynedd
LL41 3SU
www.cinnamonpress.com

The right of the contributors to be identified as author of this work
has been asserted by him in accordance with the Copyright,
Designs and Patent Act, 1988. Copyright © 2010
ISBN: 978-1-907090-23-3
British Library Cataloguing in Publication Data. A CIP record for
this book can be obtained from the British Library.

Designed and typeset in Palatino by Cinnamon Press. Cover
design from original artwork 'Couple Embracing' © Luba V.Nel;
agency: dreamstime.com

Printed in Poland.

Cinnamon Press is represented in the UK by Inpress Ltd
www.inpressbooks.co.uk and in Wales by the Welsh Books
Council www.cllc.org.uk.

Cinnamon Press acknowledges the financial support of the Welsh
Books Council.

Contents

Enough

The Road Taken

Foreword

Exposure. When you reveal all; when nothing is left. Microfictions are like that: a laying bare of language, offering us a chance to uncover what might be underneath those stark words. Prose poems too jolt us into a paradoxical world where two forms collide, exposing, perhaps, sentiments that could not have been expressed in any other way.

Bill Trüb's masterful piece 'Exposure', after which this anthology is named, seems to me to be a metaphor for how microfiction and prose poetry might work: words ripped from flesh to bone, stripped to their essence, and asking us what is going on beneath it all. Many of the pieces here ask the reader to question the world and the words each author has presented. But there is humour in some pieces, too, though often of the dark variety: 'Rothko Red', 'The Night Swimmers' and 'Scarecrow', for example, lend uneasy but deserved laughter to the anthology. There are also moments of poetic admission, of stopping to express what is going on around us, but which we often take for granted, such as the heart-stopping 'Stretched Voltage'. The sections of Sign Language, Enough and The Road Taken cover many of life's experiences and epiphanic moments, but all the stories we included here are telling us something in an original way.

The amount of submissions to this anthology was huge, and we were amazed at all the submissions' strength, their insights and their stories. This suggests to me that microfictions and prose poems are gaining popularity, and becoming more recognisable as whole and complete genres in themselves – despite their apparent incompleteness on the page. Though no longer absolutely 'new' forms, they are certainly becoming more noticeable, and perhaps more accepted. It's okay to let your writing make the reader ask questions. Microfiction and prose poetry allow each carefully chosen word to expose some of those answers.

Holly Howitt
March 2010

Exposure

Sign Language

Rosi Lalor

Sign Language

There is the noise of children on the swings, and two dogs barking, and traffic. All of these sounds fade, until there's just me and you and no sound. It might be better like this. It means everything will happen in slow motion.

I reach up to my throat, and make a choking gesture. There is no way to speak, none at all. There is a hook in there. It's invisible. I make a hook shape with my finger to indicate exactly what it is, exactly where it is. I trace a piece of string with my fingers. It reaches all the way across to the hook at your throat, like a washing line.

Now it's your turn. You open and close your hand, imitating the muscles of your neck, collapsing. The look on your face tells me how hard it is for you to control them. There is a hook piercing the centre of your voice. I think that it would be nice, in a way, to see some blood, as evidence.

You look down at the ground, and I watch you. You find a line of ants carrying crumbs, and a pink glove in the mud. You keep on looking for things to look at. Meanwhile my hands get restless. They start searching for something. They search my pockets, and my body entirely. They are looking for my keys maybe, or my heart, or a pen.

Bill Trüb

Grace

She loves only two things more than me: a gold dog called Oprah and a medicine cabinet. As a young girl, she conquered whooping cough, but her throat is still full of gravel. She grinds out sentences like 'Nothin' ain't never easy,' 'You don't know what I've been through,' and 'I don't deserve this shit.' Freckles splatter her face, an early Pollock.

She relies on clouds, names them, insists they're ancestors. Cumuli—wide-hipped and jovial—are paternal grandparents; wispy and thinly veiled, cirrus clouds are definitely from her mother's side. No, she's not crazy; in fact, she studied psychology at university. During the day, she answers calls at a crisis centre. Strangers dial from mobile phones, threatening to freefall from bridges, and she always knows what to say: buoyant, inflatable phrases that cushion the jumpers just before they crack the frozen river.

Her name's Grace. We collided at a 24-hour convenience shop this morning, 2:30am. We turned into the medical supplies aisle at the same time. I was buying condoms, being optimistic. Bundled in her arms were a bottle of aspirin, *Hello* magazine, a bag of razors. She looked like she always does—like she'd been crying. 'Do you know what it's like to have a pocketful of sleeping pills in a city that never sleeps?' she barked, folding herself into my peacoat. 'Actually, yeah,' I said, but her question was rhetorical and she wasn't listening.

We moved to the checkout counter and she crawled into her oversized purse, spelunking for her wallet. All she could find were a pashmina, a browning banana, and fingernail polish. As the cashier silently judged her, I swiped my debit card for both of us, but Grace had already thundered through the automatic doors into the shaky streets. When she finds her wallet next week, she'll pay me back in promises and we'll be even.

Renyi Lim

Flight

I still ask myself if I could ever lose you. Then again, did I ever really try?

You made me sever myself from everything you touched. Shielded by mist that matched the white of a bridal veil, I fled to a pocket of the world tucked between looming mountains and glass-calm fjords. At night, stretched across a deckchair, I watched shadowed clouds encase the stars; in my mind, you faded to almost nothing.

One evening, my landlady came to the door. 'There is a letter for you,' she said. I knew the writing on the envelope. With pebbles for eyes, I paid her to burn it.

The train took me into the mountains through tunnels where the light flickered like an old movie reel, until the air was so cold that it hurt to breathe. I sought my reflection in sheets of ice, marvelled for hours at water so undisturbed that I became confused between object and image, and which side of the mirror I belonged to. If I lost myself, you would never find me.

Then, in that candlelit village with one telephone, the stationmaster called me over: 'There is a letter for you,' he said. Nine hundred metres above sea level, you could still touch me. And so down you dragged me, all the way back to square one.

Clare Potter

Chinese Whispers

Here. A very short story about a very short man who had a very short memory. In school, he was never teased except when he couldn't remember for the fifth time that lesson the square root of 333. And it wasn't that he couldn't have calculated it, it was the fact that he couldn't remember what a square root was because whenever he went into his mind, he could not ever remember having seen a *square* root and logic should dictate a root could not be square and certainly not with that lovely oo sound right in its middle. That brings me on to sounds and the very short man; he was, in one ear, deaf so sometimes, the words going in and the words going out did a strange dance that made him sound…wounded. But of course, he wasn't wounded at all.

People in the village always dipped a knowing hat to him or interrupted garden gate chatter to tell him 'Hello' or, 'Here's some onions from the garden.' People did like him because he was likeable, but mainly, they liked him because they could tell him their secrets and sometimes these confessions fell on the deaf ear; sometimes though, they went into the open ear and made his eyebrows rise and his shoulders heavy for these saggy burdens. But, he'd never remember what exactly he was carrying or who had told him what…just these sounds coming in and these sounds going out.

One day (and no good story is a good story without 'one day'), though this wasn't a specific one day: it could have been the day you were pegging out the washing and didn't answer the phone or it could have been the day you set the house alight, but on this one day, there was a very tall woman sitting in a field. When I say she was tall, I don't mean the kind of woman you see on market day and think 'Oh, my she *is* a tall lady, I'll bet she'll never find a man tall enough to look her in the eye' no, I mean the kind you look at

14

and think 'Wow, I'll bet they'll keep *her* bones when she's dead' or, 'My God,' and run because she was, and I'm afraid this will not be politically or credibly correct, but she was a giant.

The very short man was walking in the field to retrieve something or bury something. He had a shovel and a basket of buttons and door knobs. He happened on a large shadow and looked up to see the giant lady sitting in the grasses weeping; *she* was weeping and not the grasses although it is possible they wept too. The very short man thought she looked like a painting he once had seen or imagined or was going to one day paint. She looked like a goddess. Like someone he had met before. The tears plopped down from her eyes (it's hard to find a way to describe tears falling, but here, I've only got how he heard it to go on). As she cried these huge tears, the short man put down his basket and climbed up her body, using her buttons for leverage. He hoiked himself onto her shoulders and as he whispered into her ear, curtains twitched in the village and doors were locked. The giant woman let out a belly laugh which shook the sun and settled in the valley like an unwelcome mist.

Wendy Klein

Dry shade

A problematical bed to fill was how she put it, which left a lot of scope to wonder how the problem came about and when. In her faded Greenham Common T-shirt and cut-offs, she looked too jaunty for sudden widowhood; too down-at-heel to be on the pull, though her breasts were nicely presented. She didn't seem the sort to offer her bed to a canine companion, and I guessed her to be a cat-hater or even a member of 'Abstinence Actually'. *Dry shade* she whispered to the young attendant, and the ghost of Mellors seemed to hover at her shoulder, to hint at maidenhair ferns, though a gamekeeper was probably the last thing she wanted in her garden, dry shade or not. Then she disappeared down a row of euphorbia, left me to conjure her maverick world; the delicate stepping over of a wine and poem drunk woman, her late night dance, how in the morning she might hurry to 'sent items' to check her indiscretions.

Jane Monson

Via Negativa

My mother was not Christ, but she was spat at. My father was not Christ, but he didn't always know this. The two of them met in a garden, but they were not Adam and Eve. And when my mother became pregnant, this was considered a miracle, and when pregnant again, this was nothing short of Blake's sunflower vision. But we are none of these things. When my mother had an epileptic attack, she looked like a monster. Of course, she was not possessed, but as children we didn't always know this. What she was, was spat at. Someone we didn't know turned his mouth to her as she fitted on the pavement, emptied his tongue and told her to get up. Beside her, flowers shook their heads behind a newly built wall. She'd made the bricks bleed on her way down, and narrowly missed the plaque that named them the city's best roses.

Frank Dullaghan

Nipples

I remember being surprised at their size, the dark wine roundness of them, their extension, their full-stopped shock on the snow of her breasts. Even when she covered them in the blue shirt I'd worn that day to work, I could see them watching me. They seemed more real than I was, proud of themselves, absolute. There was no way I could ignore them. They existed as an accusation, a truth against which I would be measured. I felt insubstantial, a ghost, a notion of myself, in their loud presence. Perhaps I had come as a supplicant, I thought, or a penitent trying to lose the weight of his sins, looking for something to hold onto as the bed fell away from under us and the sky rushed in from the open window.

Jenny Kingsley

The Wedding Photograph

They are leaving the church, husband and wife, tentatively walking down the stone steps. Her lace train trails the red carpet. She holds up her dress with her left hand while her right clasps his fingers for support. One can see her ankles and the white silk pumps with high heels. Her veil crowns her head. He holds his gloves, top hat and the bouquet of still fresh daisies in his free hand. The door of the Rolls is open. The arm of the grey haired, black capped driver reaches out to proffer protection in case of fall, and to receive. Friends watch, friends chat; friends make new friends; friends look for new lovers to love.

She is smiling; he is solemn, very solemn. His thick dark hair, brows and lashes face her; the concentrated darkness safeguards her body, shrouded in soft, gentle layers of pure white. They have no lines engraved by the devils of sickness and nagging prosperity, and the stress of cherishing children.

Unlike many of their peers, their love will deepen rather than weaken. If he asked her again, she would not hesitate ever so imperceptibly, as she did the first time.

Tyler Keevil

Gary Gets a Giraffe

It was my wife's idea to buy the giraffe. If she'd left it up to me, I would have bought a simple present—like a mug or a tie. But she insisted. Gary wanted a giraffe for his fortieth birthday and so we got him a giraffe. How she knew what Gary wanted I can't be sure. It's one of the things that worries me. But then, there are many things that worry me these days.

'It's a little excessive, don't you think?' I told her.

'Honey, if anybody deserves a giraffe it's Gary.'

Charlotte had me there. But did anybody—even Gary—deserve a giraffe? I never asked that question. Now I wish I had. The more I think about it the more I realize what a terrible decision it was to give in to her generous whim so easily. But that's exactly what I did.

The expense, of course, was enormous. It wasn't merely the original purchase, but all the extraneous fees that inevitably cropped up: the shipping, the duty, the housing and care of the animal. The bills have only just begun to settle on my desk like so many lifeless moths.

Still, money isn't my main concern. Two weeks before we gave him the giraffe, Gary came over for dinner. He brought sushi and wore the kimono he'd picked up in Tokyo. He quoted Basho. Listening to his voice, and seeing the saki-induced rapture in my wife's eyes, I had the horrible premonition that this giraffe wasn't the last thing she'd be giving him.

I'd hoped that once we'd presented him with the animal my fears would be alleviated. But it's impossible to forget the scene at the party. Charlotte had wrapped an enormous red bow around the giraffe's neck. The men from the zoo delivered it just as Gary cut the cake. Everybody gathered round. Officially the giraffe was from both of us, but it was obvious—to Gary and the rest of them—that it was Charlotte's brainchild. He thanked me in his usual, exceptional way, before he gave Charlotte a hug and asked her to walk the giraffe with him. They paraded up and down the block, the rest of the party in tow. All the other guests said it was a splendid idea for a gift—just what Gary needed. My wife, of course, was ecstatic.

My own birthday is in three days. Charlotte hasn't yet asked me what I want. I won't know what to tell her if she does. How to explain that I want something bigger, something better, than a giraffe? I can't just resort to sweeping generalizations; Charlotte will want me to be more specific. Gary is always specific in his tastes, his opinions, his likes and dislikes. Worse, I'm plagued by the fear that Charlotte won't ask me at all. She won't ask because she already knows what to get, has perhaps already purchased my present and wrapped it neatly in generic paper with white ribbons. The more I think about that, the more likely it seems.

I just pray it's not a mug or a tie.

Tania Hershman

Straight Up

My father was not a slouching man. Every night when he finished dinner, he pushed back his chair and sat up straight as a rod, the way he did when demonstrating posture to his class of teenage girls at our school. He drummed his fingers on the table, tap, tap, tap, and looked at me, my shoulders, my slumped neck, the way I was shovelling mashed potato into my mouth, and I felt the heat of his discontent. He jerked his head upwards, and this was the signal. I was to instantly drop my fork and, as if some invisible cord was sliding through my spine and out the top of my head, I was to ascend. My shoulders lifted, my neck unkinked, and I grew, and as I grew, so his face softened, his brow lost its furrows and the corners of his lips lifted. He would nod his head back and forth, saying nothing. This was how it was every night. This was how it was on a good day.

I saw my father teach his class only once. I was supposed to be ill, supposed to be feverish and damply sweating into the over-washed sheets. But I was a faker and good at it. An accomplished liar by the age of ten, I knew the tricks, thermometer against light bulb, moans and groans. My mother, who couldn't miss a day at the factory, set me up with juice, water, a pile of comics and instructions to call if I vomited but otherwise to stay exactly where she left me.

Of course, I didn't. I got dressed after I heard the front door slam, sidled downstairs and stood, breathing in the empty house, the sweet smell of freedom. What drew me to the school? It should have been the furthest thing from my mind. But I was pulled in that direction the moment I left the house.

Like a spy, I slid along walls and around corners. When I got there, I crouched beside the window of the room I knew he was teaching in. Slowly, slowly, I straightened up until the window sill was at eye level and I peeked in.

At first he didn't look like my father. The context was so strange; it was as if he was in front of one of those painted movie backdrops. He was pacing backwards and forwards by the blackboard upon which he had drawn a spine, with all its vertebrae, moving up into the neck and head. The girls were clearly not very excited about whatever he was telling them. I saw two of them passing notes, a few were chewing gum, none of them was sitting up straight. He didn't have them; they weren't eating out of the palm of his hand, not at all. They put up with him, as if he was a lost dog sniffing around their feet, but then, when the bell rang, they jumped up, grabbed their bags, streamed out of the door. And I saw my father standing by the blackboard, by his perfect drawing of a spine, standing up as straight as he could, and I could see in his face that he was hoping, straining, for some kind of reaction from them. But the girls didn't even see him. I was the only one. I was the only one who saw him standing there.

Sue Wood

Shiva's Dance

I don't remember much about Harrow-on-the Hill Registry Office. It's a modest building with easy parking around a late fifties cube of steel-held glass and unobtrusive swing doors. As for detail, I have forgotten it, or there was nothing else to remember. It made no civic or architectural statement. It was designed to be forgotten: a flash of glass in a photograph behind a new bride's smile, catching just enough light to give her an up-lit glow.

Like its municipal partner, the crematorium, the Registry dedicated itself to processing significant human events. The swing doors turned singles into couples.

Inside, the building was cheerful, clean and carefully secular. I think it was divided up into four or five service areas. A fat man in a brown suit checked the groom's name and waved the whole wedding party towards a numbered door. Unlike the endlessly spacious holding areas of crematoria where grief must be isolated from grief, here parties could mingle. They could eye each other from under hats and mascara, uncertain if they were strangers, relatives or gate-crashers on an alien wedding group. Only the brides stood out, a *cordon sanitaire* in their tight bright faces. The fat man occupied himself separating strangers out of wedding groups with the agility of a sheep dog. If there was bewilderment on a face he had penned expertly against a wall of pink and navy outfits, then he pointed to a waiting bride by way of quick reassurance.

The wedding room was like a classroom in a new school. Or it might have been a big lounge or a sales persons' training centre with a semi-circle of soft chintzy chairs. Years before my own marriage day, I had looked through a window into a Hindu temple in Katmandu. There was a chaos of dancing. Energetic food-throwing engulfed the two still points in the temple: Shiva frozen in his Wheel and the bride turned to a stiff gaudy confection in gold and silk.

Another suited man indicated where we were to stand. He pressed a button on the side wall and a young woman cruised into the room. She was hugely, ripely pregnant. We heard our friends stir behind us. The second suited man read his way through the ceremony, pausing in the most unlikely places. He was tapping into memories of a parson. Now he acted out the role with slow relish, mispronouncing words with an unfailing knack. Behind us our friends almost giggled. We could feel them biting their lips.

And then the unborn baby started to dance: bo-ing, bo-ing, bo-ing. I stood inches away from its mother's belly and watched the tiny half-feet capering up and down under the woman's tight silk dress. Each movement seemed a dimple in an arc of unseen water; the Lord Shiva imprisoned in his Wheel dancing the universe into light.

'Do you take this woman...'

Outside we saw a bride standing alone at the bus stop holding her wedding train over her arm. We have a photograph to prove it. And here's this one of us both, twenty-five years ago, outside the Harrow Registry Office. There's Bobby fishing something out of his eye, my dead Aunties and Uncles, baby Mark running into the road, Nanny who put all the spare HP sauce sachets and sugars from the Reception into her handbag, my mother looking anxious, my father looking absent... dancers all, behind a darkening glass.

Catherine Smith

Vow

For Jack, the final straw comes on their twentieth wedding anniversary in the Boar's Head. Heather, his wife, drunkenly puce-faced, tells all their friends that her husband's such an uncommunicative bugger he might as well not speak at all.

At this moment, he vows he'll never speak to her again. It seems less complicated this way.

It takes Heather a little while to notice.

'There's no way I'm cooking tonight,' she announces, pouring a large glass of Chenin Blanc before flopping onto the sofa, 'so either shift yourself or ring for a takeaway. I've been in meetings all afternoon and I'm going to take it easy. I'm sick of running round after other people.'

Jack crunches an apple and flicks through the *Radio Times*. He works as an engineer for British Telecom, fixing faults. He's eaten a large portion of lasagne at lunch-time, anticipating that the question of dinner would be tricky where only one person was discussing it.

'Did you hear me?' she asks, glaring at him.

He points the remote control at the television. On the news, a reporter talks solemnly into a microphone in front of swathes of police tape; teenagers are stabbing each other in North London. The camera pans back - flowers in cellophane wilting along walls, little white cards scrawled with messages—*Why you?* and *Desi, you r sleeping with da angels now*—all because one boy looked at another in the wrong way, or said something, or this boy thought that boy said something, even if he didn't.

Talk is dangerous, thinks Jack, tossing his apple core into the bin, and even when people don't talk, but look at each other in the wrong way, that's dangerous too. He takes his coat and heads out of the room.

'Do you want dinner or not?' shouts Heather from the sofa.

He clicks the back door quietly behind him. He walks down to the river and listens to the water gurgling as it rushes past; the wind rustling the willows as they sigh and sway.

By the next day, Heather's texting his mobile, ringing him at work to demand to know why he's not talking to her. He finds her voice increasingly tiresome. In fact, he finds the voices of his colleagues, with their wittering about bonus schemes and holidays and train services, almost as bad.

Inside his own head, he likes to listen to his own thoughts.

He writes her a note on the third evening; *Have decided not to talk to you because you don't listen.* She tears it up and scatters the pieces all over the table. He makes himself scrambled eggs on wholemeal toast and pours himself a beer as she weeps, noisily, and then rings her sister. She's on the phone for nearly two hours. He watches a programme about the French Resistance on the History Channel. He learns a lot.

A month later, she initiates divorce proceedings. *Unreasonable behaviour.* She tells all their friends he's impotent. And mad.

The old friends are no longer in touch. He deletes their numbers from his phone and scrubs them out of his address book.

He attends an evening class to train as a signer for the deaf and meets a quiet, thoughtful woman called Jennifer. In her bed at the end of term—candles flickering and wine on ice—she looks deep into his eyes, signs erotic fantasies to him as he gasps with pleasure. He loves to work out what she exactly she means as she presses one finger against his lips.

Mark Ellis

Somebody Get Me My Coat

She'd been vegetarian from before we met. Tried vegan but gave it up after a year or so and settled for vegetarian. She said she hated the way it made her feel. Not physically, she hated the way that people she met thought she was on some sort of crusade.

'Nobody notices vegetarians,' she said.

I guess I agreed. People always had to tell me they were vegetarian. I never believed them at first then I started noticing the way they grumbled about the choice when we went to restaurants. I was never friends with vegetarians for very long. It was raining when she rang on the door. It was a Sunday and I'd put a chicken in the oven. I do that about twice a year. She stood there soaking wet. There's that song, Tracks of my Tears. Is it Elvis? UB40? Somebody. You can't see his tears because it's raining. I don't even know if it's that song. I fucking hate that song. This was a bit like that. She stood on the doorstep and I could tell she was upset.

'Jamie called it off,' she said.

I told her to come in, offered her a coffee whilst she sat in the lounge and turned the oven down. When I came back all her clothes were in a big pile on the floor and she was lying on the sofa. She didn't say anything to me. I took off my shirt and trousers. I took off my boxers. She didn't say anything as I got on top of her but she pulled me in, wrapped her arms around me and started kissing my face. All I could think about was the pile of wet clothes on the floor. I stopped and I remember the look in her eyes at that moment. I got off her and went to put her clothes in the dryer. When I came back, she'd left the sofa. I looked in the two bedrooms then found her in the kitchen sitting on the floor in front of the oven. The door was open. She was just tearing strips off the chicken and forcing them into her mouth. Just forcing them in. I stood there watching.

Rhys Hughes

The Moon and the Well

Once again, the moon is setting behind the old well at the bottom of the garden. Our slack faces crowd at the window, noses pressed to frosty glass, eyeing the falling moon. Lower and lower it sinks until it has completely vanished. Once a month we wait for this moment, we ache in the silence. At other times, rocking on our wormy chairs, rubbing our bony knees in front of a dying fire, we seek to fill space with songs and timid stories. But no words can emerge from our drooling mouths. We need the laughter of a child, the warmth of youth. We listen for the sound, the splash of water that will redeem us.

Together, trembling hand in hand, we race down the garden path, dragging our nets behind us. We have not been deceived. Our long wait is over. The moon has missed the horizon and fallen into the well. We pull up the gurgling moon in a bucket and plunge our nets into the depths. The moon struggles beneath the silver liquid, a ladder of moonbeams rippling on the waves of emotion that sweep over us. It is a very new moon. From now on, the nights will always be dark. In the corner of a ruined cottage we will set up a cot. Through the bars of this cot we will feed our lunar child with a long-handled spoon.

Sarah Hilary

I Cannot Carry a Tune

I've taken to collecting sheet music. Anything and everything; it's a cheap hobby. Most of it I find in charity shops and at car boot sales. I've filled three boxes with famous scores and nursery rhymes, pop songs and violin solos.

I'm tone deaf.

It's one of the things you said you loved about me. I can't read music any more than I can play it. It makes me sad. You always said it shouldn't, but it does.

I cannot carry a tune, no matter how I try. And I do try. Not operas, I wouldn't dare, now I haven't you to go with. Just little things, jingles on the television and radio, *musak* in supermarkets when I'm queuing to pay for a bag of oranges.

'Music can be orange,' you taught me, 'or blue or green. It has a scent and a colour. You don't need your ears; let it in through your other senses. See it. Taste it.'

Your tune was the colour of pomegranates, with the same quick bright flavour, surrendered one note at a time. It is in my fingertips. It fills my palms and dances under my skin. I carry you with me everywhere and it makes me lighter, and it makes me less.

So I sit with my boxes of sheet music and I search for you there, the sound and smell and taste of you. I think—if I could piece together enough sheets, the right sheets, I could make a whole.

Your curves are in the clefs, and in the empty eyes of notes. I've searched and I have found you there.

Lynda Nash

Panderage

'Stop pontificating,' she told him curtly.

He accepted the tea she'd made in a cup that hadn't been pre-warmed, grinned toothlessly and said, 'You don't even know what that means.'

'Yes I do!' She looked at him indignantly then went to the spare bedroom. From behind a secret panel in the wardrobe she selected the *Illustrated Dictionary For Bored Housewives*. As she ran her finger from 'polyandry' through 'pompous' and 'poniard' she wished she'd married Thomas. A milkman's wages aren't as much as an English professor's but they would have always had strong teeth.

Kachi A. Ozumba

The Devil's Lies

You clench your fists so tightly that your fingernails bruise the soft centre of your palms as you shout AMEN!

'Yes, with God all things are possible,' the immaculately dressed man on the podium says. 'But watch out: the devil is a liar. He will seek to sow doubts in your mind and rob you of your deliverance. Resist him! Just believe and receive your healing: Cancer, I cast you out! Barrenness, I banish you! HIV, I unhinge you . . .'

The AMEN you scream as HIV is unhinged is so forceful that your throat burns. You gasp afterwards and fill your lungs with air charged with hope and desperation.

You open your eyes and look: the born-blind is blinking and reading from posters that adorn the arena; the diabetic is dancing and rejoicing before the cheering crowd, the lame is laying aside rusty crutches to walk with hyena-gait before the white banner proclaiming deliverance from all yokes of the devil: poverty, stroke, and other such afflictions.

A feeling of lightness grips you and your body tingles. This could only have one meaning: you too have been delivered!

But don't you need a test to confirm this?

You are quick to recognise the enemy's attempt to sow doubts in your mind. 'The devil is a liar,' you mutter, and jump up to proclaim your healing.

Your feet glide over the road as you head for the Lagos Bus Station, smiling through the early harmattan fog. You sit between two passengers whose bodies poke and press upon you like a vice. Had you not abandoned your old ways, you would have cursed and sworn that they had half-eaten chicken bones hidden away in their side pockets. You smile at them instead and call out, 'Let us pray,' before the bus begins the twelve-hour journey back to your home.

Your wife opens the door and runs into your arms. You bury your face in her hair, revelling in her familiar smells. You move your hand to her tummy.

'It's not yet visible,' she says, and assures you that your first child is growing well.

She serves your food and sits opposite you, full of questions about your fourteen-week border patrol posting. You know she is staring with surprise as you close your eyes to bless the food.

In between mouthfuls, you tell her how much you missed her but do not mention how you touched yourself during the long nights while dreaming about her shapely hips; you tell her about the drinking parties but do not mention how you had ended up in the arms of a prostitute after one such party, or how she died a few weeks later from the big disease with a little name. All that is in the past and you are now a new creature.

Finally you tell her about the crusade but not what had driven you there, and you invite her to share in your new life.

Dutifully, she agrees; anything to please you. She turns up the light of the kerosene lamp and notices you have lost weight. You tell her you have been fasting for the crusade but do not mention that, before that, you had been in an involuntary fast, induced by your test results.

You spread out on your bed after dinner. Your body trembles with longing as you listen to the splash of her bathing. She joins you in bed, clad only in a wrapper which she casts off as she falls into your arms.

'The devil is a liar,' you mutter, as your bodies become one.

Robin Lindsay Wilson

Cain's Defence

My brother Abel has comb-over hair. Under his tongue I used to see a silver key but that was before he won the Primaries. I never saw a jackal in his eyes until he was elected.

He declared war on TV but he never spiked a cocktail, or stole a motorbike. Abel never could choose a law to reject.

I applied for the job of walking his dog. Never had a reply. He believes power and pastel cardigans are synonymous. I applied for a job as his food taster but the Lackey-In-Chief wanted a police check and an imagination with an on/off switch.

When my brother was sworn in he declared peace on sweatshops and impresarios riding tiger economies but tattoos and canvas shoes were banned inside the Oval Office.

I applied to be his bodyguard but was chased by the FBI across the three worst states and back against the White House gates.

His press conference in slacks and gold bar moccasins was the last straw. If he had asked me for a nose stud, a tab, a joint, an E, a needle or a buttered choirboy, he would still be in power. I guess he had some trust issues. I can confirm his worst mistakes. The half net curtains and the Rockwell prints.

I would have saved his life if he had helped me burn the picket fence. Killing him was an accident. I trusted him to escape when I loaded the gun. It was his imagination that let him down.

Jeremy Worman

Lotus Flower and Cherry Blossom

Windows rattle. A May morning in Mehetabel Road and the rain swirls the litter. A twittery laugh makes me jump.

At the other side of the road a pretty Vietnamese girl is standing under the large cherry tree. She stretches for a branch. Her boyfriend's thin arms embrace her waist. She jumps. Blossom falls on their heads, which they brush away in a dance of fingers.

'Come on Minh, come on.' She pulls on his arm and giggles.

'Wait, Nhu, wait,' he says in a breezy, singsong London voice.

A flash of sunlight illuminates the nearby English trees and bushes that seems to burst into Vietnamese life as grapefruit and banana, papaya and peach flower, orchid and water lily.

Nhu and Minh kiss. He holds her tight, she wriggles free, bends on her knees. Her arms are in half moon above her head and she rises in white jeans and top to unfold like a lotus flower.

He steps back.

A car backfires, their heads turn with a quickness of fear, strange to watch. Their people's history seems to shadow them: two million starved by the Japanese in 1954, the Vietnam war with its outrages and napalm, the communists retaking of the South, the journeys of the boat people, some of whom eventually landed up in Hackney...

They smile again and skip together down the path.

Wendy French

My Friend and My Invisible Husband

He's there, a shadow just inside the hallway. Caught by the light through the door frame. Transitory like reflections in the wind whenever you come round. Even when you've stayed all night you believe he's not there. Two empty coffee cups on the kitchen table mean nothing when you come down for breakfast and the front door closes. All you see is me staring at our neighbour's brick wall. You wonder how long this silent pathologist inhabited my imagination. How long can he remain? Last night at 3am you thought you heard footsteps prowling around, pacing the landing but by four all was quiet. No shoes or razors remaining. On New Year's Eve he gives me the last glass of champagne, leads me to bed. Turns out the light. Bolts the front door against strangers.

Mary Carroll-Hackett

The Real Politics of Lipstick

She learned the secret authority of her mouth at a young age, too young to form the words, but she understood the looks men gave at the innocence of the Tootsie Pop in her lips, a generous mouth her mother called it, easily sliding from a smile to a sulk, that ice cream cone a weapon that she wielded easily by the age of fourteen, the sweet cream of it deliberately left on the cushion of her bottom lip as she watched them stare, sweat, shift away from their wives. Look up at me, look up at me, they said, and she did, especially after she discovered the ultimate power of lipstick, blood red for regular guys her age, who wanted to rush, wanted to own the cleft of her upper lip, the tangle of hair they fisted at the crown of her head, but she switched to blushing pink for older men, that sweet slow youth they struggled to remember, cotton candy, candy apple smeared across her cheek as they mouthed thank you thank you thank. They all thought they were taking her, as she knelt, eyes lifted, thinking of nothing more than how for that moment, she owned them, branded each forever with the tip of her tongue, shadowy traces of lipstick that would never completely wash away.

Bill Trüb

Pick-up Line

Just wondering if maybe you'd like to grab some beers sometime, maybe at Duplex down on Christopher, maybe anywhere this side of the International Date Line, wherever singles go to splash conversation, like anvils introducing themselves to puddles, with people whose names are lost in the bottoms of pint glasses then found between twin sheets, people who tell their life histories in one breath, but can't tell a tree trunk from a toothpick, a traveller from a tourist, a man from a man, people like you and me—who only like people like you and me—Scorpios in the sky, Scorpios in the sack, wide-eyed, wild, one-eyed jacks in a deck of hearts, brother brain cells crushed by the crown of a philosopher king, still wondering if, maybe, we could shed our muscles and make-up long enough to make sense of ourselves under an honest constellation.

Enough

Bill Trüb

Exposure

In a grove of twisted citrus trees, naked men and women thrash each other. They lust for the perfect combination. Men with horse thighs find women who spread like peacocks. Their bodies clap in the soil and they pant in unison. They deep kiss until their lips disappear and they're lapping a slit on a face. Everything their tongues taste flows into their mouths. They suck each other down, her navel then his. His nipples, the nape of her neck. His abdomen flakes like salmon and her breasts bust. They scoop out eyes like melon balls. They swallow each other's throats. Their skin sheds and exposes tender tendons. Intestines entangle and choke the life out of innards. Blood lubricates the slipping and pounding of snakes in foxholes. One thousand pelvises collide until flesh is pulverized into powder. Soon they're just bones raging on bones, ribcages shattering, femurs bashing like baseball bats.

On the outskirts of the grove, hidden cameramen put down their equipment and masturbate to what's left: a crop of hearts fucking like dogs.

Jane Monson

The Clock

The head of the man in front of me clatters with rage. Above him a china plate clock on the wall, the hands of which haven't yet moved from summer to winter. 'Get the cake,' he says. The woman doesn't answer, but tilts her face towards the ceiling to finish her glass. A small white round object tight with icing and coloured by letters appears. It is lit with six candles, and hovers above the palms of the waitress, her mouth half open as everyone starts to sing, her voice the unsure body of a child's first dive. When the song is over the boy leaps onto his seat and grimaces over the orange flames. It is his birthday and he is going to take time blowing out his age. He is not talking, but cackling; flinging his neck back and widening his eyes until their glow dims in the vanishing light. At the last puff, he picks up the knife and slices the cake under a small cloud of smoke. Everyone gets a letter. The man in front of me gets his own initial. With his left hand, he forks it, brings it to his mouth, and swallows it whole. His head stops shaking as he focuses on the wine; the way it chases the lump in his throat. In a minute, a thought will leave his mouth by accident.

Rachel Eunson

Footprint

Three days later, she made it as far as the vegetable yard. The potatoes that he had planted still there under the heavy, cold soil; still nourishing her. But the potatoes would only last so long, and then they would be gone too.

Then she saw the footprint. She watched it; moved around it delicately as if it were an injured animal that might flee and also be lost.

A faded box of Polyfilla, half used on some long forgotten repair, waited under the sink. She mixed the whole box and sat beside the footprint in shattering breeze and salted sunlight. She looked out at the greasy sea and remembered, all afternoon.

After dark in the warmth of the house, she compared his Wellington boot with the cast. Then his walking shoe. Looking down to see if there might be another pair of shoes that she had missed, she saw her own muddy boots. She removed one and held it beside the cast. An exact match.

Heather Leach

The Things I Didn't Do

I didn't sleep with a woman. I kissed one, a girl, my best friend. Jane. More than once, deep kisses on the mouth, almost tongues, her breath hot and fast on my cheek. Her parents' bedroom, but on the bed, not in it. The two of us back from school while the rest of the family were out at work. Sun coming through slits in the curtains, summer made us hot and more dramatically inclined. That's how we explained it to each other, to ourselves, we were actors, performers, still children pretending to be other people: princes and princesses, Romeos and Juliets. Sometimes she was the boy and I was the girl, then the other way round. In this way we kissed, every day deeper, every day sweeter. That's all. It was a close thing, very close, but no, I didn't sleep with a woman, never once pulled back from the acted-out kiss and opened my eyes so that I could look at her properly, really look, at her skin, her thick brown hair, her lips.

I didn't marry a man called Michael or Carlo. Nor a man who was a farmer or worked in a shop or had red hair. So many husbands I didn't marry, didn't meet, didn't love, yet there's one I think of the most. I was getting off a bus on my way to work and he was getting on. We didn't even see each other face to face, all I caught was a peripheral glance, the side of his jaw and the quick shift of his shoulder as he pulled himself up onto the platform. I think he was wearing a dark leather jacket but couldn't quite see and as the bus ground past up the hill I didn't even look at the window. I never saw the childhood scar on his thigh, never held his narrow white body in my arms or tasted his smoky mouth. All my life I missed him, missed his eyes turning to look at me, my hand on his sleeve.

I didn't work in a flower shop or a crematorium or a factory. Didn't become a shop steward, never led the comrades out of the gate to the cameras outside. Didn't become a boss or a miner, a bird watcher or a singer. Never smashed the state, never tried cocaine.

I didn't invent or discover anything, no scientific breakthroughs, no cures for cancer, no anti-gravity mechanisms.

I didn't hit anybody, never felt teeth against my fist, never drew blood, although I wanted to. I didn't murder anybody but I thought of it. Perhaps if I'd married the man on the bus, I would have learned violence. There was something in the way that he turned, that sharp angle of jaw that told the whole story, how it might have worked out. Long years of silence, two of us in the bed staring up at the ceiling.

I never discovered what it was I was supposed to find, the secret, the answer, not even the question. The child knew once, but she forgot. I didn't taste oysters. Never saw the Nile.

Lisa K. Buchanan

My Palatial Estate

Closet space is a coveted commodity in this town. When my co-workers at the bookstore learned of my newly acquired closet, they became jealous, dropping to a murmur in my presence and pondering the source of my good fortune. Had I received a secret pay raise? Inherited a million? Snuggled up to a rich fellah? The rift was greater still when it got around that mine was no ordinary closet, but a spacious walk-in with a hardwood floor. 'Does the butler serve high tea?' a co-worker asked, surmising that only a lavish flat would feature such a closet. And yet, the 'palatial estate' I reputedly inhabited was a sweet deal, renting for only half of my monthly earnings, and I wasn't about to let anyone's envy drive me out of it. Wouldn't others snag the luck if they could?

At first, the teasing was gentle and I assumed the interest in my new place would subside. Then, in my personal cubby, I found a flyer from a professional closet organizer and a subscription coupon for *Metropolitan Home*. One co-worker introduced me to a customer as 'our Upscale Living Specialist.' Humour turned to ridicule; query to interrogation. I detached like vitreous from a retina. No more Crucify the Customer; no more Skewer the Reviewer; no more after-work drinks.

Then, one slow evening, they cornered me. Yes, I admitted, my closet still had its Edwardian brass hinges, rosette knob and inoperable skeleton key. Yes, its egg-and-dart mouldings remained fashionably intact, like the embossed wainscoting and exposed copper pipes. And, like many late-Victorian closets that had once housed a toilet, mine still had its double-hung window—painted shut, I added, hoping to mitigate the sighs and swoons my description had elicited.

'And your room mates?' someone asked.

'Shoes make the stenchiest bedfellows,' I offered. 'My clothes take up more than half the space and I'm always getting my hair tangled in wire hangers. This morning I nearly forged an eyeball kebab on the hat hook.'

Nobody laughed. Customers tapped; the phones wailed.

'And the reading light is pathetic,' I added, certain that this, of all hardships, could not fail to impress.

The store manager's lips formed a perfect square. 'You,' she said, 'have a walk-in closet all to yourself. Cut the whining.'

Later, it was suggested that I improve relations by hosting a party, but I was convinced that once my co-workers actually saw my closet, they'd envy me even more. Plus, I can be rather particular about my home. I don't let people eat or drink in there, and I worry that someone might scoff at my no-smoking policy—did I mention that the window is painted shut?—and burn a hole in my bulky, dominating, wool coat.

Eventually, I got another job. Now when people gripe about the lack of closet space, I just nod my head and gripe along with them.

Amy Mackelden

The Librarian

Sounded like she'd been saying it since she got born—'This is due back in August.' She's not specific anymore because no-one ever is. Jack says, 'See you at ten,' then he's there at ten-thirty. Days don't make a difference, or days don't make as much difference as you think they will once you've grown up.

When she says it to me—'August'—a slight hiss on the S because she's bitter at turning twenty-six and still working here, I watch her eyes move across pages, her hand as it stamps every book in my pile, pushing each aside as if it's yesterday's newspaper. Really, it's older, written in the sixties by authors that are dead, and I'll relate even less to their words than I do to hers.

She says 'This is due back in August.' But what's overdue is more interesting, because that's what's unravelling. Her date stamp is running out of ink.

Rob Carney

Contests

My old roommates weren't competitive; they were nuts. And not just about tennis, about everything. Boggle. Ping-Pong. But at least that makes sense, you know; you keep score. No, what I'm talking about is I come home one time, and they're in the kitchen arguing about who's got the best vertical leap, only there's no way to prove it since the ceiling's so low. Anyway, my guess is that Casper, or Zee, it doesn't matter who started it—one of them jumped up and slapped the ceiling, so then the other one had to and so on, 'til they wind up jumping and trying to hit it with their heads. And that's when I walk in. I walk in and these Olympics are already in progress, and I get drafted as judge. Seriously. What I'm supposed to do is decide whose head slams into the ceiling the hardest—best three out of five. It was dumber, and also a lot harder to judge, than it sounds. I mean, they made up all these skill points to consider: like the sound of the impact was a factor, whose neck showed the most recoil was a factor; things like that. So Casper goes step-jump-*boom*, and Zee goes step-jump-*bam*. And the two of them are actually doing this, knocking their skulls flat, ragging on me that I'm a crappy judge when a call doesn't go their way. Now, this all happened years ago, and I can't remember who won, but I guarantee this: if those two idiots were here right now, they'd both swear it was them. Zee would be sure that it was him, and Casper would go, 'Dude, you're out of your mind.' And this would keep going back and forth, back and forth, 'til they'd finally have to have a rematch.

Laura Tansley

She Settles in Scotland

She came from the South with traces of boys whose visits soon petered out. So she decided to try boys from the North. She dated these boys, drank whisky and Coke with them, drank enough to kiss them at the end of the night, it being rude not to. She became friends with most of them, tension being what she sought. Tension that made her hair and skin glisten; the promise between friends of a line being crossed, from neck to navel, breast to breast.

She was jobless, but enjoyed all the free activities the city had to offer. Tennis, bowls, street theatre activism, writing camps; free fillings because she was on the dole and her teeth were full of holes. She started clubs of which she was mostly the only member. The letter writing club was started because the interviewer at Peckham's deli had been so patronising, *Don't you know what's in tapenade,* so she wrote an admonishing letter which she posted in a box right outside the shop; laughing yoga, to cheer herself up; subway dance club because the flashmobs looked fun in London, but when she and a friend tried it, they kept banging their heads on the roof of the toy-like trains.

She read a lot. The library was where she met Euan, a chess player (another free activity). Tall, awkward and purposefully provocative, he would say things like, *'so why are you even here', 'if you're so creative, why can't you get a job', 'I don't think we should be friends', 'I love you'.* She kept dating. Once she went out with an artist who couldn't afford to take her anywhere, so he bought an apple and a banana from a greengrocer's for their lunch and took her on a walk around autumn suburban streets. He'd no interesting stories to tell but she let him put his hands in her anyway.

After a few months, the call of the South was too strong. She was tired of making an effort, so she decided to move. Euan had suggested reconciling at the beach before she left; it was a bright-green day, so she got in his car and they drove out. He stopped at a house at the side of a B-road, seeding grass around the front door, ivy in the hedgerows. His parents were renovating it. The living room and kitchen had dustsheets over the floors, the single glazed windows that showed a view of a garbled back garden had mould growing around their edges. Upstairs, a double mattress had a single sheet spread over it. 'Did you want to spend the afternoon here?' he said. 'I don't think so,' she said, manners escaping her for once.

He dropped her off at her flat so she could pack. She had three charity shop wedding dresses in a bin-liner that she wasn't sure what to do with. He sat in his car, one hand on the wheel. He didn't look up at the bay widows of her living room that rattled when the front door closed, that had shaken when he pushed down on top of her on the sofa; that sang when cars drove up the street. She peeked at him through these bay windows, every-so-often, as she went through the flat dividing up her belongings between her housemates: rugs and clothes, paintings, home-made plaster-of-Paris stepping stones, face-painting kits, water-proof playing cards, an antique hair brush and hand-mirror. He stayed there for a while, one hand on the wheel. In the shower she thought about decorum, but by the time she was dry he was gone.

Jenny Adamthwaite

Shell

Here's what I did: I broke the egg into a small red bowl and whisked it up with a splash of milk. I melted a bit of butter in a saucepan and slipped some bread in the toaster. I poured the egg into the saucepan, cracked some black pepper into it and whipped it around with a wooden spoon.

The toast popped.

I spread butter on it and poured the warm, crumbly egg over the top.

I stepped over your legs. I sat down. I realised I'd forgotten to make a cup of tea. That's when I cried.

The kitchen was so cold I could see my breath.

I couldn't see yours.

Non Prys Ifans

Grandmother

We knew of no one else who had lived to such an age. She was as blind as a mole, but could still freeze us with a stare when we tried to steal her Imperial Mints.

She taught me how to write, made me press the shape of letters into the crepe of her arms with my firm fingers, the imprints staying for weeks.

In the last days, the hair in her ear holes had grown so ferociously we had to liquidize our words in the food processor and pour them into her ears through an enormous tin funnel.

When she finally died, her death rattle goose-pimpled the whole village.

James P. Smythe

Primitives

Tess takes her hand off the wheel for just a second, but that's a second too long. The car in front brakes, suddenly—to let the driver shout at her children on the Jeep's back-seat—and she doesn't see it until it's there in front of her, kangaroo-bar through bumper, through boot, into back seats. Both cars lurch forward, one driving the other, until they stop, shuddering, hitting something. There's blood. Jordan, Tess's son, is unconscious, which, she thinks, is good; he hates blood. He's breathing. He looks fine. Tess opens the door, stumbles to the road, onto the white line in the middle, along it like a drunkard testing their level for the police.

'What did you do?' she screams at the other woman. The bit where their cars meet is meshed. Tess reaches for the door handle twice before she gets it, and pulls it open. 'What did you do?' The other woman is bleeding from the head. Tess paws at her face, moves it around to look at her, but her eyes are rolled backwards, all one colour, a trudgy brown; the blood that had been racing along those tiny veins in the eye over-spilled, the yolk bleeding into the white. Tess looks to the front of the car and sees what stopped their momentum—a lamp-post, cut through the bonnet and held there, a knife in a wedding cake posed for pictures—and then looks to the passenger seat. A young boy—too young to be up there, that's what the law says, in the back until they're sixteen now, she thinks—is pressed against the front, slumped down, a deflated air-bag against his face. He's covered in blood from his—Tess assumes—mother, the crown of her head, she now sees, split open. His throat is just as deflated—crushed—as the airbag. In the back of the car are two children, both smaller than the one up front, only three or four. They're asleep, or the other, hunched forward. 'Doesn't bear thinking about,' Tess says aloud. She staggers back to her car and grabs Jordan.

They stand on the side of the road and watch as the police and firemen and ambulances appear, as they put clamps over the doors and wrench the cars apart like they're made of Sticklebrix. Three minutes later, the paramedics give up and head towards Tess and Jordan, checking their pulses, leaving the rest to stew on the side of the road on their stretchers. Nobody fusses their bodies until their sheets are pulled from the ambulance.

When they get home, Tess's husband, Tony, has cooked. Jordan sits at the table, mildly concussed, and pokes at his food. Tess eats everything put in front of her then asks for seconds, then wonders if there's anything for desert. She eats the entire Vienetta, then sits for hours on the side of the bath, vomiting, shouting excuses through the door as Tony puts Jordan to bed.

Kate L. Fox

Addiction

He rolled the carpet into a giant cigar and started to smoke it. The shag pile burned well enough and gave him a pleasant high. He defrosted the fridge-freezer and melted it down on a teaspoon. The kitchen table and chairs broke up into powder that went straight up his nose. He drank the three-piece-suite. The house finally empty, he started to pick at the walls brick by brick.

Angela France

Timing

The man you can set your clock by doesn't own a watch. He passes the corner at 7.26 every morning, metronomes his arms to an insistent tick and whisper you can't hear. He turns away from the town clocks, averts his eyes from the clicking numbers on the bank wall, concentrates on his customers. He stamps cheques, nods to the next in line. Stamp. Nod. Stamp. Nod.

Commuters don't register the first missed morning. The bank manager cuts him some slack after fifteen years with no sick days. He doesn't call. Days later they look for him, find him curled in a tangle of springs and spindly hands, empty faces moon down at him from every wall. He doesn't speak, doesn't move, except for his head. Twitch. Nod. Twitch...

Angela Readman

Snow

The snow is falling. That's all it does now. The snow falls everywhere, all the time, soundless as apology.

'This is a nice place,' I say. She talks about paints, all their colours. I nod, like a man who sees them, a man who knows the difference between antique white and porcelain. All I see is snow. Her tasteful room fills with static like we are both within the tank of a badly tuned TV.

'It's really starting to fall,' I say, walking to the window. She hands me a glass, ice cubes jangle and crack as if something is breaking out of their freeze. She talks about window treatments, how the place is maybe too much for one, wants me to know she's not much of a cook and wants me to smell what's in her oven and compliment it anyway.

I've heard of scenes like this: the first invite to an apartment, a preview to see how someone lives their life. Cushions freshly plumped up, easy chairs for me to imagine every night of my life in. In her attentiveness to her guest, she wants me to see how easy she could make things. How there'd always be good coffee and wine. She lights the fire, it crackles and sputters to wake.

'Better to be in, on a night like this,' she says, staring at the space beside her on the rug as she warms her hands, like a man is missing from its design.

The fire does not melt the streets outside. The snow keeps going, always. White as tomorrow and a long time ago. I drink my brandy and its flame hits my gullet, topping up brandy's of winter's snowed and thawed. The taste is mingled with a name, creaked from my lips, cracking as someone a lot like me stopped the car, ran towards a lake, following small footsteps, a trail of thoughtless words I'd exhaled into the air that chased a girl like a ghost was on her heel. It was dark, except for the light of snow. The girl stepped onto the frozen lake. Fell to escape my hand on her arm. I did not push; I reached for her hand, to catch an impression of me I couldn't let go.

The woman with the apartment asks if I'd like to hear some music and puts on a blizzard of jazz. Outside the snow keeps going. I watch it cover buildings, twenty one, twenty three. I count the buildings until they are lost to snow.

'It's nice, not to have to talk all the time, just be comfortable enough to enjoy each other's company,' she says.

My head knows how to nod, my face can smile in the right places, between the flakes. She talks about silence. The snow falls outside, over buildings, in the room between us. She talks until we are both covered in snow.

Brian Baer

Silence

We heard you walked down to the basement and held the cold barrel beneath your chin. Your parents still have pictures of you throughout the house, but down there, the only thing to remind us of your presence is that small hole in the ceiling.

We rolled out our sleeping bags below that mark in the old drywall and lay still, staring up all night. We never spoke. I don't know, maybe we thought we could hear from you down there where you had stood, that maybe you would do the talking. We had questions, and your parents avoided the topic as a kind of make-believe coping method.

Dawn slowly rolled over the horizon, brightening the basement through a small window nestled against the ceiling. Our ears had become so trained in the moonlight that we picked up every creaking floorboard, every wind gust, every breath from the person next to us, and could, if only for a second, pretend it came from you.

As we could hear your parents moving around upstairs, we all sat up and looked at each other in silence. We had come to you for answers, for explanation, but again you had told us nothing.

Collin Tracy

Neighbours

The neighbour died at night. Or: the body was found at night. The neighbour died at night or the body was found at night. The body was found in the evening really but the neighbour probably died sometime during the day. Or in the afternoon. Yet, it could have been the night before. The neighbour died, and at night the next day — or the same day — the neighbours gather on the back porch of the small apartment building. The neighbours gather under the light and stamp on roaches. They smoke cigarettes one after the other and drink warm beer out of bottles. The soft brown dog — the dog of the neighbour who is dead — runs into the yard looking, looking. But the neighbour is dead. Not only that, she is young and dead. The neighbours gather there the next night too. One neighbour uses the death as an opportunity to hug all of the other neighbours for very long intervals. One neighbour uses the death as an opportunity to have sex with the other neighbour. One neighbour goes home and can't stop thinking about the silence next door, on the other side of the wall. This neighbour presses his ear up against the wall and listens. He feels uneasy at night when all the other neighbours are asleep. This neighbour lies in his bed, half-drunk, with tears running into his ears. He thinks about how when his neighbour died, he was just next door. He was right there, right where he was tonight. He was her neighbour. What had ever separated them? Wood. Plaster. Sleep. And now this. There are four neighbours. Well, now there are three. The neighbours gather on the porch again on the third night after the death of their neighbour. They are running out of steam. They all have deep rings around their eyes. They try not to look at one another in the porch light. Tonight there is a grill going. The locusts are vibrating in the tree by the apartments. Tonight it is warm out. Tonight there are some other friends and some other dogs. And tonight there is her mother. Oh god, sweet Jesus, none of them had thought of it: of course there is a mother.

Sheila Killian

Fish

His first word after the long silence was 'fish'. I don't know why—a dream maybe? If there were dreams. He had opened his eyes two days earlier—stared glassily then slept again. He seemed at ease, not scared by the fluorescent lights and monitors. I stayed in the black plastic chair by his bed, drank tea when the nurses brought it round, walked to the canteen with my daughter when she came with her dad. I was neglecting her, I knew that, but still I couldn't go home.

I think it was ten days he slept—breathing shallow and easy, eyes so closed it seemed they would never open. The drips and drains did everything for him; the nurses tended him like an orchid—light, water, stillness. They tended me too—told me nothing, but with confident, professional smiles.

The consultant came by twice a day drawing interns behind in v-formation. Sometimes he spoke to me, mostly he looked through me and described the coma on the bed. He didn't see a child there. One day he joked to his students, and referred to my boy as 'Lazarus in waiting'. I willed him to look at me, to meet the fury in my eyes, but he didn't. One student did though, and had the grace to look away.

He lay there, thinner and longer than in life. Did you hear how I said that? As though he were dead. I can say it now. Truth is, he seemed more dead than alive those long days. He was laid out on that white bed, still and beautiful, unbruised. I could hear people at a future funeral telling me how peaceful he looked, that it was a release, that the good die young or some such bullshit. It played in my head at night, a beautiful service, but too short.

But instead, he opened his eyes and spoke. Fish. Then other words from the holiday place, and his sister's name, and so far it's all flooding back to him, through him. The storm in my stomach is settling a little. I'm able to eat. I think he will come back from these lost days.

But I won't, not fully. I look at him and I know he can be gone any moment. When I remember his coma, I see candles, smell lilies by his bed. I've lived through his death, and that changes everything. How can I love him as much as I should now I know he's not mine to keep?

Fern Bryant

The Answer

It was weird in this day and age, but I didn't know my real mother. I think every kid has the right now to find out, but I didn't know how to go about it, and the woman I had always known as my mother wouldn't say a thing. In fact I didn't know anything until I was thirty-one and Aunt Evie let it slip one day when we were having lunch in the pub. She didn't use the word 'adopted'. She said, 'after they took you in'. In from where?

By that time my dad was already dead from hypertension. It took me months before I got up the nerve to ask her, but one hot afternoon as I was helping her dig in the garden, I spit it out: 'Mum, who's my real mum?' I plunged the spade into the earth right after I said it. There was a long silence. Then she cleared her throat. 'We won't talk about that now,' she said. I let it go. I had to.

Months later, in the kitchen, I said: 'I need to know, Mum.' She put down the drying-up towel slowly and said: 'Not now. I'll tell you when the time is right.'

I was flummoxed. What could I do?

As it happened, two months later she was diagnosed with breast cancer. By the time they caught it, it had already gone into secondaries.

Every day I would sit by her bed in the hospital, willing her to tell me. She'd mostly lie there with her eyes closed, in her own world.

She didn't have long to go, and one afternoon I said to her again: 'Mum, I need to know.'

She looked at me then, and her eyes travelled to the bedside drawer. Then, slowly and clearly, she said: 'It's in there. Everything you'll ever need to know is on that tape. Just promise me you won't listen to it until after I'm dead and buried.' Her fingers dug into my flesh like talons.

I reached into the drawer, and just like she said, there was the tape, with my name on it. It was like a fairy tale.

'Thanks, Mum,' I said. But she'd already slipped back into her own world.

I floated through the next few weeks. She died on a Friday and the funeral was the following Thursday. It went off without a hitch. I was sad but elated.

Everyone came back to my flat for coffee and sandwiches. They all said the expected things, and I nodded in all the expected places.

Then they were gone. But I didn't rush it. I threw away all the paper plates and washed up all the cups. I even brushed the crumbs off the table.

Then I poured myself a whiskey, got out the tape, dropped it into my cassette player, and listened.

It was empty. All ninety minutes of it.

Wendy Klein

Coffee

You lie in your new bed, fake maple. You are nearly seven and the smell seeps under your door, hijacks the morning with the promise of breakfast, but the promise is always unfulfilled, like the first taste of it—bitter. You should learn, they all say, to take it black; experience its purity, but all you can think of is your insides, all pink and welcoming, surprised by the deluge of darkness from your father's tilted mug, the sting of it on your lips, the tang and burn on your tongue, tart, disappointing like when your auntie let you taste cocoa without sweetening—lessons about the unexpected, about how nothing ever fulfils its promise, the let-down, like love.

Bill Trüb

Piñata

The morning sun lassos a ray around my neck and hangs me.

Parents blindfold their children, spin them three times, then slip oversized branches into their palms. 'Play nice,' they say, as the kids take turns whacking me. They send me swooping in twists and twirls across the sky. Sometimes, when I'm hit from both sides at once, I'm sandwiched still.

By midday, parents tell their children to stop beating me with oversized branches. 'Aluminium drainpipes,' they recommend. They smack me red-raw. After several hours, the children's arms tire and they stop beating me with aluminium drainpipes.

Parents then grab their children by the ankles, tell them to stay stiff and use their kids to beat me.

Finally, I break. The neighbourhood rejoices in the sun shower. They snatch straight from the air and stuff their faces. They want me so bad I almost mistake it for love.

'Mmm, I got a failure tear!'

'Not as tasty as my queer tear!'

'His ugly tear tastes like peppermint!'

Soon the moon, fat as a bull, charges the sun. The ray unravels from my neck and I freefall to Earth. Empty, I smack concrete without making a thud. Up and down the street, kids suck puddles dry through straws.

My ulcers will crowd their potbellies by sunrise.

Valerie Bird

Pearls

The birch tree is still here, leaves fluttering freely in the smallest breeze and the bark peeling back to a whiter beauty. And underneath my guilt is buried.

'For my granddaughter, Sunday's child.' The golden girl; to her she promised the pearls, one gleaming strand, so perfect, like her. And who was I, skinny, dark and Wednesday's child, full of woe? 'There will be something for you,' she'd say, 'There's no need to be jealous.' But she, my big sister, would always be bonny, blithe, good and gay. Until the day she died.

Granny wore the necklace on Sundays, the iridescent sheen, the creamy glow accentuated on her pink and crumpled neck. Laying them on her dressing table at the end of the day she would say; 'They must cool and breathe before I put them away.' And away was a black box lined with velvet and I wondered whether the soft dark would be like the oyster from which they came.

I didn't take the box. I wrapped the pearls in tissues and a plastic bag against the wet. The ground was hard but I dug deep with a little fork beneath the tree. It was late and I was brave and no one found me out.

Leukaemia came to bleach the Sunday child, the white overwhelming the red blood cells, they said. I didn't understand. Though I knew that I was even less the one they wanted when she was gone. She, only eight, they said again and again. And at six I believed that if I went and she came back they would be happy. The pearls were nothing to worry about then.

Granny lived with us always, as long I can remember, and when my parents died she was still there for me to care for. I found a home where she told the story of how the pearls disappeared the day before her darling granddaughter died. Again and again, and the other old people looked at me, the dark sibling, with pity.

I sat by her bed in those last hours as life slipped gently from her. I held her hand as she talked again of the pearls; 'Precious they were but not worth the loss of love.' And I kissed her cheek and whispered that she was precious to me.

Alone today I stand beneath that tree a fork in my hand. Above me sheets of discarded bark curl back to reveal the sheen of a new trunk, the leaves rustling, frenetic and sad.

I bury them all. The pearls can never be mine.

Herbert Williams

Insider

That's better. Much better. No more pain now. Can't move though.
    Silence. Except for. Steady drumming. Funny.
    Resting. Just resting. No-one shouting. Questions.
    Must remember. What found out. When I'm let out.
       Must tell them. Straight off.   Important.
    Where are they. The others. Can't hear them. Silent.
    Must remember. All that happened. Hostage.
    Words fading. Can't remember. Must remember. That.
    Drumbeat louder. Quicker. Boom-BOOMING. Sliding. No …
NO.

WHITELIGHT. Voices. Hurting. HITTING.
Get … word … out.
AAAAAAAAAAGH!

Rowyda Amin

Sanatorium

So light he hardly dents the mattress, my grandfather breathes with half a lung. Moths, unseen by the nurse on night duty, flutter down from the curtains and hover over his open mouth. Feeling the breath become weak, they wind silk reins around the iron bars of the bed. They tense and tug the strings to prepare for the moment when the breathing stops. Then they will drag the wheeled bed through the double doors of the ward, out the front entrance and up, over the car park, to the hanging lightbulb of the moon.

Gail Ashton

Saying It (All)

I

The sayings of Dad, not to be confused with those of Mother, involved language. Cobs that he sweated and which we had with cheese and onion for tea. Working his roe out all week so mom could have some with chips on Fridays and did we think money grew on trees? He was often too jiggered to go out dancing after all those jiggery-pokery goings-on at work. She went on her own. We've nothing in common, she said. He was all goalies and goolies, jimmy riddles and jacksies, and seeing men about dogs. He could often feel the toe of his boot up your backside, specially when she came in late.

She taught us to read and the names of all the film stars. From him we learned that having your arse in your hand was not the same as knowing arse from elbow. That you could stick one on someone— your mom's fancy men (he said)—or have one on you for days (she said). He had something on your bloody mother but he never told us what.

His middle name was Horace. We gave it to our toy pig while his back was turned.

When she finally goes he doesn't say much at all.

II

My mother often went to the foot of our stairs, for no particular reason, and sometimes all round the rakin—which was actually a place called the Wrekin according to Dad but what did he know (she said). She knew of blue murder everywhere, specially in supermarkets, the need for clean underwear and hankies, just in case. In a minute someone would feel the back of her hand and a certain someone needed to get out from under her feet, for god's sake, and let her breathe. She could bee-bop and jive, fag-and-

72

coffee-it all day long, or tuck her arm through ours and squeeze-hug, for no particular reason. He trailed her round the house singing *please release me* till she threw the roasting fork at him and told us get your coats girls. Another time she upped and left without us. We sat look-out on the stairs forever. Just in time to do my tea he said when she walked back in to a house with no lights on. Your father has a face, she said, as long as Livery Street: and who could be doing with that?

On the morning of her funeral we pull on brand new pants and leap around to *Jumping Jack Flash. Everything I own* is on someone's car radio. Traffic is murder (she'd say). We laugh like drains when Dad forgets the house keys and scrambles over the back gate to let everyone in. He tells us to shutitjustshutit in front of all those people.

Every night we wait at the foot of our stairs. Just in case.

Rothko Red

K. A. Laity

I fell apart one day in front of the Rothkos in the Tate Modern. I recognized in a shrill cry despair and a wordlessly howling grief, but I did not recognize it as my voice at all. There had been no sensation of the sound rising or the power that drove it. I had been quietly sitting on the bench as was not an uncommon habit for the afternoons lately. It was the way to while away my free time since losing my job.

My lover, Keith, had disparaged me for it. 'Why aren't you looking for work? How are we going to keep this flat if you don't have a salary?' I would dutifully check the job listings each morning, circle likely prospects, and then lose the paper somewhere between our flat and the South Bank.

Sometimes I would go watch the Surrealists' films, taking up valuable cushion space while others stood, sighed and eventually moved on. But most often I would go to the Rothkos, soaking in the dark canvases and the sombre lighting which nearly always hushed those who came through the doorway, enforcing the contemplative spirit of the works.

Today had seemed no different than the several days that had gone before it. Perhaps it was the rat, lying by the quayside in the low tide—bloated, abandoned, a carcass. As carefully displayed upon the shingle as a Beuys' Vitrine, it was framed by a Curly Wurly wrapper and a Starbucks cup, lying on a short plank. The wood had been greyed by the river's patient sanding and staining. It contrasted with the rat's piebald colours. In its way, it had been beautiful.

I wondered what had killed it—or even if a rat might take its own life when all hope seemed to be past. They were intelligent creatures after all. Is suicide a measure of intelligence, I pondered later as I drank in the heavy red of the paintings. The red on the canvas before me seemed as dark as menstrual blood, that monthly reminder of having failed once again. The black rectangular shape within the blood marked a pollution like drunken diarrhoea.

I was not aware of being particularly bothered by these thoughts. It was just another day in the Tate, until I heard that shrill cry. It filled me with panic, but I didn't know how to stop it. People were staring at me, but I couldn't move. I just sat there, gripping the seat of the bench with my straining fingers. After a time, as a crowd gathered, security came and the very nice woman pried my fingers from the wood and the quiet gentleman shifted the crowd aside.

A small girl cried, tears streaming down her pinkened cheeks. It made me sad that she might associate art with pain, so I smiled at her as they led me by. Sometimes a small act of kindness can do so much.

Jane Monson

Church Falls

The roof quotes Gothic, then Romanesque. The floor understands neither, its aisle stone tongue cracked and splintered, each flag its own fit. The ground looks starved. Rugs are cast like bones; the dips and folds make flesh or skeleton of the faces that pattern the cloth. Each look is of a tight or a loose order according to the flow of the weave. Smoke contorts above the fabric, then cuts out and sinks into the design. Incense fills the unstitched gaps. Stutters from the organ mark the air. The minister opens his mouth as if to yawn, falls away from the lectern; static returns in his voice.

A marble falls from the pocket of a boy and tells us where the rug ends and the stone begins; he lifts another to his smile and swallows it, tugs at his mother's sleeve. Tugs again.

Frank Dullaghan

Mug

The mug sits on the table. That's what it does. That's all it does. It does it well, solidly sitting in its mugness, its handle an open ear able to catch all conversation, if there were any conversation. But there is none. The mug sits on the table alone just as I sit on this chair alone. A little while ago, I held it softly in my hands, my fingers pressing their tips against its spine, its ear nestling against the stretched skin between my right forefinger and thumb. Everything was fine then. But something suddenly went wrong. I will never understand mugs. Now it sits on the table, empty, silent, as if it has forgotten what we had going for us, as if none of that matters at all.

Jo Swingler

A Remembering

It's October. Her mother is drowning slowly in a hospital bed three hundred miles away. The doctor calls when something new happens, something new that shifts her mother down a notch, sends her down another step, but there is nothing she can do. There is no up, even though the doctor hasn't stated this is in the black and white terms of medicine. There is no up, only this inevitable incremental sliding down towards whatever exists afterwards, if anything does.

She thinks about this 'afterwards.' Considers it. The afterwards for her and the afterwards for her mother. What it will be like when her mother no longer exists. What it will be like when the one person who has been there forever is gone. It is a feeling of something she can't grasp. A slippery feeling. A feeling that shifts and alters itself into allusive, swimming forms. Eludes her and floats round to the back of her head where the dead memories lie. There isn't a function in her brain that can process these thoughts. Her life has always contained her mother.

But then, very soon, it doesn't. There's a phone call. Her mother is officially dead before the doctor calls, but there is that moment where she's not. That not-knowing means her mother is still alive. It is only the knowledge, that phone call from the hospital that kills her mother. Without it, her mother exists.

There are times when she goes to dial her mother's number on a Saturday morning to share the stories of her week; things the dog had done, something funny, stressful, irritating from work, the ten pounds she'd won on the lottery, the new coat she'd seen in town that she probably shouldn't get but wants to just run it by her mother first. But her mother wasn't there. There was a falling away. It wasn't this huge aching grief, but a sharp grasp of breath, a small shock. A remembering.

Phil Madden

Mermen Were Lonelier

Mermen were lonelier. There weren't so many of them. He could swim for months and not see another. Sometimes he swam close to the mermaids, just to have contact, however unacknowledged, like a face on the edge of a crowd.

This was how he met her-looking for them at the end of the estuary, just before dusk.

He'd never seen humans there before. And no one so beautiful.

She'd always loved mermaids. Had often seen them, just out of sight. Saw the ripples as she rose from her dreams. But this! This creature was magical.

At this point in such stories it is customary for there to be a spell-for a wish to be granted.

It happened here, too. Their yearning caught the eye of the wandering gods who give blessings at whim, the way humans reward one beggar and not another.

But different gods.

Her wish was to change her essence, to become a mermaid, so she could be with him, and the wish was granted.

His wish was to become a human, and this wish, too, was granted.

Phil Carradice

Snitch and Snatch

We called them Snitch and Snatch, two old women, each of them replete with skirts like billowing sails and whiskers that our pre-pubescent chins could never hope to emulate. They haunted all our childhood dreams.

We knew that they stole children, kept them hidden, cold and starving in their cellar—though, naturally, none of us could be precise or offer dates and names. It didn't matter. They were our perfect demons.

And yet, despite the fear, there was no risk we would not take. Nothing could stop us hounding, cat-calling 'Snitch and Snatch' whenever they came near. Or knocking, pounding on their door in Gas Works Lane—even the name seemed right—then running as they charged, skirts flying and with banshee wails that followed as we fled.

Until one died—we could not say which one. Snitch—or Snatch—lived on, shuffling her painful progress round the town. We did not bother her. Only as a pair, one entity, could they exist and now their power was broken.

Except, for years, we could not meet the milk-eyed gaze of that survivor; ashamed, not by what we'd said or done, but by an emptiness that struck, as sharp as daggers, into the space below the rib cage. We'd watch her go and silently, consistently, she stared us down.

One fine day, she seemed to promise, one fine day...

Valerie O'Riordan

Enough

They shared a heart, the doctor explained, and lungs. They curled towards each other, telling secrets, a language of tangled veins and mingled blood. Nobody else knew what to say. The mother unravelled tiny blankets, refused to eat, listened to the awful endless pumping of her own heart. The father, in an empty apartment, strung up the x-rays: a row of flattened ghosts, hanging from a clothes-line. Echoes of his wife's cheekbones, his own long fingers. He traced the crooked arc of an impossible rib-cage. He whispered their names into the silence.

Michael Spring

Long Road, Few Trees

It was a long way to come. A long way, for one whose life had been so insubstantial.

The car park was full of people. A few were friends but mostly they were those I hadn't seen for a while, barely recognised. Most looked ravaged. Some hid bitterness with difficulty. A few smiled comfortably. Gradually, expressions and voices came into some kind of focus, recalling empty moments in pubs and bars.

We shuffled in to the crematorium. It was new, pine-panelled, a chilly space without life or dignity.

There were awkward readings, a song or two. Someone was crying loudly at the back.

Her sister thanked us for coming. She didn't seem to have changed much.

I recalled the brief affair I had with her, years back. She and her husband hadn't been getting on. I had simply been there. Why had I done it? Had it just been one more attempt to be close to the one I couldn't have? I hadn't thought of that at the time.

I had a glass of wine and a sandwich back at the house, but I couldn't look her father in the eye, an old man now who, quite clearly, had other things to think about. Her sister was back with the husband. They both said something to me, but then went outside where their teenage boys were struggling on a rusty climbing frame.

A life had ended, but not their lives.

It all seemed a long time since I had rung the bell of the house and she had come easily to the door, saying, 'God. You're early,' as though there was so much time ahead, so much time that it would be stupid to live in anticipation. In that moment, everything had started to crumble.

What had she been wearing? I didn't remember. She would never be photographed, and now, every day since the phone call when I had been told she had died, her features had been more difficult to grasp, slipping slowly away in my mind, as though she was melting and there was nothing I could do to keep her for myself.

Over the years, we'd kept a sporadic friendship just about alive. Sometimes I imagined that she might once more look at me with the ice-blue fire in her eyes, but I never truly saw it.

I walked down to the river. 'More of a ditch than anything,' she had said once when I had journeyed up to see her. She had abandoned me that night too, leaving me at the bar with a blowzy woman with red lips while she disappeared, her phone pressed to her ear.

Now, I lit a cigarette and looked over the flat landscape. Rich earth, reclaimed from the sea. Wind from the north. An occasional willow, looking lost in the vastness, almost embarrassed to be there.

I stopped in the nearby town on the way back. The town where we had both grown up. The lights were on now. A few people were out, looking in the shop windows. I walked past the place she had hit me once. The catch on her bag had left a small scar on the line of my chin. Later, I saw the bridge where suddenly she had stubbed her cigarette out on the back of my hand. That mark was still there too.

It was a long way to come. A long way to come and stand alone.

Rowan B. Fortune

The Mannequin Maker

The mannequin maker went to buy the raw materials for her doll's construction. She went to the shop and bought what she needed to make the doll's legs. On her return home she was run over by a passing driver and used the material to create prosthetic legs. The next day the mannequin maker went to buy the raw materials for her doll's construction. She went to the shop and bought what she needed to make the doll's arms. On her return home she was run over by a passing driver and used the material to create prosthetic arms. The next day the mannequin maker went to buy the raw materials for her doll's construction. She went to the shop and bought what she needed to make the doll's head. On her return home she was run over by a passing driver and, losing her head, died.

Tina Barry

Velvet

Seven days. Dad's not coming back. Seven days of Velvet and Mother, folded together, lovers. I open the door to her room, just a crack, dust motes like dirty planets whirl over their bed. They wince, startled. 'Go!' she yells at me. I stare. The hair we loved to comb is a nest of snarls; her eyes belong to a sleepwalker. 'Go! Go!' She reaches for the blanket, the Chihuahua, as tiny as a bonsai, curled against her stomach. I linger outside her door. 'Mom,' I say, hoping she'll call me back. There's no answer.

Bloop. Velvet's paws hit the carpet. The new man of the house is on the prowl for food, a walk. Breakfast was Rice-A-Roni; for lunch I'm serving Ring Dings. Perhaps he'd like a bite? Now he's cornered: me on one side, my sister on the other. 'Herrrrrre's Velvet!' I say. He's a miniature Johnny Carson in a thin fur coat. 'Herrrrrre's Velvet!' my sister mimics, her voice sweeter and softer than mine. We laugh. Encouraged, Velvet emits a yelp: Oh! He's forgotten we hate him.

Beneath my arm, he's made himself as heavy as an old stump. Our neighbour waves as we rush past. Two girls and their dog. She can't see him quivering like a divining rod. Neither can the drivers who pass us with benign smiles, their thoughts on chores, dinner. We turn a corner, away from homes where housewives watch, away from traffic. There is a cement bridge no higher than my waist; below it a stream bounces over small rocks. 'Look Vel,' I taunt, lifting him over the side. He's frozen, then flailing. I wish his brittle nails would tear a hole in the sky, a hole my father could walk through. 'Stop!' my sister shouts, 'He'll fall.' He's safe now, grateful, his silky head nuzzled beneath her neck. Our strokes are calming, gentle. We murmur 'ssh,' and 'now there,' and 'it's okay.' Words we remember and miss.

The Road Taken

Robin Lindsay Wilson

Under Other Orders

He has a lance, a brocade uniform and a bulge. Broken pillars are not his concern. He knows without looking her breasts are bare. Soiled brickwork infects her suckling child. There is a distant city but she is between storms. It is not his baby. He would help her if she were closer to a doorway. Without reason his hard-on arrives. Lightning passes between the clouds. Brocade deceives him into believing he is attractive. The column he leans on has been struck by lightning many times. His fear keeps the woman behind a grey silhouette. The electricity finds its victim. A hard-on gathers blood from every act of selfishness. He does nothing. The master is in ruins until an order comes.

Maria Winnett

Have You Got Some Fire?

After the comment I had made a few days earlier, when Maureen Pepys's flat went up in smoke I felt for a moment that I was responsible. The implication was there in the way her arm draped over the fireman's shoulder, her nails smudged and painted purple, the knuckles calloused but dripping with rings that were five pounds a piece from Argos.

We'd been standing in the courtyard earlier that week, both enjoying a Silk Cut Light in the evening sun, when she'd started her usual teasing. From anyone else I would never put up with it, but as Maureen and I had no connection besides being smoking pals and living in the same block in Streatham, her self-appointed role of salacious friend crossed with scolding mother was something I tolerated with a mixture of amusement and stoicism. On this occasion it was simply annoying. She'd seen me returning late the night before, not alone, and was trying to extract details, none of which I wanted to spill. I kept trying to change the subject. 'In France,' I said, 'when you want to ask for a light, you say, *Tu as du feu?*' I focussed on the burning tip of her cigarette. 'And it literally means, *Have you got some fire?*'

This only made her chuckle.

'I bet you were getting some fire last night, young madam.' She took a long draw on the cigarette and I watched the end quiver, defying gravity before it crashed onto the paving flag.

A few moments later I heard her laughter turn into a hacking cough and realised this gave me a chance to escape: I offered to fetch a glass of water and, nodding, she threw me the key as I dashed indoors.

In her flat, on the ground floor, the television was on. The faded pink of the wallpaper, the reflection of the antique mirrors, the damp washing, all gave me the feeling of being on the inside of a tin of Spam. The cigarette smoke that lingered in the upholstery was as old as the stains on her fingers, for she came outside not for fresh air but for company. Looking through the open door to the bedroom I saw library books on the dressing table: Georgette Heyer, Jackie Collins, Mills and Boon. On the floor was a bottle of gin and an ashtray filled with cigarette ends, and with an urge to close the door behind me I hurried outside to give her the water.

When the fire alarm sounded a few nights later at 2am, like most of the residents I was asleep. We gathered in the courtyard in various states of undress and bad temper, muttering and speculating about the cause and severity of the blaze. But as the fireman emerged carrying Maureen, dressed in an evening gown, wearing enough lipstick to make a whore blush, she caught my eye and called out with a film star smile, 'I got some fire!' My guilt was misplaced: in setting the place alight she had got exactly what she wanted. With her hair done up she looked like a buzzard in a wig, but her face, caked in Max Factor, was agitated and radiant. Hanging onto the fireman's neck as he set her down on the grass, she made her way across the lawn, waving like royalty. I smiled and waved back as she made her way through the admiring crowd.

Matthew Hedley Stoppard

Vice-Prefect

Slipping a magazine from his schoolbag, Shane closed his bedroom door with his back until he heard it click. He flung the schoolbag to the wardrobe corner, reached across his window to draw the curtains, and shut out October and neighbours emptying rabbit hutches, pegging out washing. Once the outside was forgotten Shane placed the magazine on the bed with the cover facing upwards and knelt down to lean on the mattress. He produced a carefully folded wad of tissue from his pocket and placed it beside the magazine.

He had got the magazine from Wiggy.

There was no one in the house. Shane had inspected the garden shed for his uncle's bicycle; it was gone therefore his uncle was tending his allotment. There was a yesterday's shepherd's pie in the oven, which his auntie, before he left for school, had advised he eat for tea. Shane had locked the back door, closed the living room door, so that he could hear it if someone were to walk in, and he had half an ear listening for the creaking banister on the stairs.

'Filthy Housewives and Mature Whores:'

Shane thumbed the first few dog-eared pages—Wiggy leant magazines to lots of lads—and loosened his trousers to drop them about his bent knees. Peeling down his boxer shorts Shane scanned the central pages to find a woman he liked: a blonde with snarling lips and cellulite like spat out chewing gum—*no*, another blonde with a blunt fringe and smelly looking stockings—*no*, and a dowdy auburn-haired mother posing by a washing machine—*no, no, no*. All shoddy photography: badly lit.

Shane unwittingly turned the page to the elderly ladies section. He choked at the sight of rolled loose skin and wrinkles; the mismatch of perms and lingerie, risqué limb positioning that prompted arthritic pangs. There was one model with a homely face *Your grandfather wasn't a big drinker; he would have a few pints of bitter and whatnot when Christmas came round. It was smoking his pipe that did him. I wouldn't let him smoke in the bungalow, so he'd smoke when he walked the dog. Some days he'd walk it five times so he could smoke more. All his clothes stank* fingering her vagina through frilly knickers.

Shane's eyes veered from the magazine and onto the square of tissue he had planned to catch his ejaculation then to the in-growing hairs on his thighs and the clumps of red running-track gravel on the carpet that had crumbled from his school shoes. *and so did his fingers. He stopped straight away when he was told he had throat cancer—that's why YOU mustn't smoke! You don't realise when you're doing it, that you're hurting yourself. But, like I said, he didn't drink much. He enjoyed it, not to excess. Even towards the end, after they had cut out his tongue, we were driving past a pub, around Christmas time, and your grandfather tapped the window, to get our attention. When we were looking at him he started pointing at the pub ever-so enthusiastically. He smiled with his mouth closed.*

The magazine closed. Shane pulled both his underwear and trousers up and picked up the tissue to wipe his nose on it. Wiggy would get his magazine back tomorrow. Meanwhile, Shane retrieved an olive-coloured exercise book and an English Anthology from his schoolbag and began his homework with his back leaning on the radiator, beside the bed, under the window.

John Freeman

Heretics

Why am I watching this, I thought, this programme about the Amish? Lovely people of course, this family, but caught between one set of preposterous beliefs and an even more preposterous set they're being ex-communicated by the bishops for breaking away from. Still, they are hard to forget. Of their sick child, facing three years of chemotherapy, the young mother says, if God takes her hand in glory that's—these were her words—fine with us.

They have such open faces, clear, quietly smiling. His is long, strong, and handsome, framed by hair all round like Robert Browning—it's the style, but suits him better than most. Imagine Robert and Elizabeth reincarnating as Amish! I can't forget the love in his face when he tells his son on his seventh birthday, I like you because you are my son—I'd settle for that cool word if it went with a look as warm as that.

Above all I remember his saying to camera, trust means he isn't going to worry. They could ruin these three years with worrying and at the end their daughter would be cured or she wouldn't, but having worried wouldn't have made the difference. Preposterous beliefs. He tells his son he wants him to be a teacher, and bring other people to God. What a seventh birthday present! All the same, what a family. She's expecting a fifth child. They have given away the money from the sale of their farm. What will become of them? I see his strong face, unclouded, not worrying, smiling at the camera.

Rowan B. Fortune

Ebony White™

My favourite is Ebony White™. What is Ebony White™? What is Morning Mauve™? Cream Whisky™? Ruby Fog™? Sexy Amethyst™? Dewy Blue™? I was given a form once and one of the questions was, 'Occupation?' What do I write? I invent names of colours that don't exist and apply them to colours that do? I wrote, 'Advertising specialist'.

I'm not complaining. I like my job. I am a contemporary poet, considerably wealthier than the older poets. You disagree? I don't qualify? Why? What I write is beautiful; it is aesthetically pleasing to a lot of people to believe that their walls are Burning Blue™. It is also fiction. I am a published poet. Catalogue #32 features thirty fully illustrated pages of my work.

You think, perhaps, there is no technical skill? I use assonance (Ochre Orchid™), alliteration (Jazzy Jasmine™) and rhyme (Lilac Black™). There is a certain irony to some of my pieces (Light Night™). Admittedly the imagery is hard to conjure (Sapient Green™) and the word limit restricts me from repetition and enjambment, but I make up for this with elegant simplicity (Pallid Ice™). My favourite is Ebony White™. Don't you wish you had thought of it?

Mark Rutter

The Archaeologist

We see him crouching in the sand, towelling dust into a sieve. And who are we? We are the winds of Oryon, and we have whispered to him in his sleep, all of these years, telling him the secrets of our waterless world. But we have misled him.

His beard is white, his hair is thin, we have watched him age through the lonely decades, digging in the husk of a dead civilization. He has given his life to our planet, although the more cynical among us say he has given his life to nothing more than a dream—a dream we fed and watered until it filled his every waking thought. Still others say it is the mirage of his pride and vanity he chases amid the dunes, and we merely provided him with the materials needed to build a palace in the sands of an alien world. In his own mind he is a saint of science, say the more malicious of our throng, and we have tempted him with seductive phantoms merely to take amusement in his torment. And yet there are those of us who take pity on the lonely old man, scratching at the rind of a desiccated rock, searching for answers to questions he has never even acknowledged.

Twenty-four days past the summer equinox. Searched the northern perimeter of the city and found what I think may be the remains of a palace complex, or at least the entrance to one. Most of it is buried under dust and sand, but the recent storms of midsummer have shifted the dunes eastwards slightly, uncovering a large anteroom or reception chamber, apparently covered with frescoes—I haven't managed to clear an area of wall large enough to be sure as yet.

We see him asleep in his bed, dreaming of his masterwork: *The History and Destiny of the Oryon*. If only he would open his eyes—should we whisper it to him?—there is a new constellation in the black sky outside his window. It hangs there for a moment, then one by one each star streams down into the dunes at the city's edge. Is it the dream or the nightmare of every archaeologist to meet the ancient people they have devoted their lives to?

96

Tomorrow morning he will find the streets thronging with noise and bustle as the work of repair begins, for the Oryon have returned, to reclaim their birthplace and examine their booty.

When he awakes to find his 'enlightened ones', his 'tribe ultimately too refined for physical existence', fawning over coffers of jewels, weighing bars of gold and platinum, coveting the oiled and perfumed flesh of captives, will he love them, these vanished people returned, or will he prefer the creatures he imagined? Those dead children, almost—he has felt such tenderness towards them—will he be able to endure them in the flesh?

Susan Richardson

From 'OS Explorer 10'

Grid Reference 8841

As drives go, it's been fairly daring. From blue line to red to orange in less than two hours, a regression from motorway to B-road that's given her a tingle like the symbol for a viewpoint in her gut.

He follows her directions to the white 'P' on the blue background, parks, and springs out of the car to explore the cliff top. She walks with more caution, swaying a little from the force of the wind and from having to sidestep sheep dung and clumps of gorse, objects too small or impermanent to feature on the map. Otherwise, the scene from the crest of the cliff is just as she expected—in fact, she's been practising the oohs and ahs that the three-mile stretch of sand demands from the moment they joined the B4247.

He steps away from the cliff edge so he can take her photo and she smiles the pecked line of a footpath—anything more solid is an impossible task when the map she's still gripping is all a-flap in the wind. Photographing him is even trickier—while she struggles to grapple with both zoom lens and unruly map, he poses, arms outstretched, as if laying claim to the span of beach way below. She's used to him acquiring a bit of a swagger when they go for Sunday drives but it's usually unfenced tracks less than four metres wide that have this effect, not comparatively major B-roads.

Just as she steps towards him to hand back his camera, the wind decides to swagger too. It snatches the map from her fingers, flings it into the air and hurls it over the brink of the cliff into a blank grid square.

At once, her head silts up with the symbols for gravel pits and scree. For a moment she stands frozen, unable to believe what's just happened, then turns, gulps and stumbles over wind-thrashed grass back to the car.

Rummage through boot.

Yank doors open.

Scrabble in seat pockets.

Check parcel shelf.

Slump on back seat.

How to survive a journey minus eyes flicking between map and windscreen?

Where else might the Ordnance Survey substitute be?

Glove compartment? No.

Think. Stay calm. Breathe…

Only when he comes sauntering over to the car does she remember. The AA Road Atlas sprawled open on the bed but out of her reach. His whispers. *Glasgow to Fort William. Cromer to King's Lynn. Bridgend to Oxwich Bay.* His insistence that she recite the right routes or risk punishment.

Not once did he trace the blue lines on the underside of her wrist with his tongue or stroke the bony byway of her spine. Not once did he deign to linger at the place where the road runs out completely.

Janet Jennings

The Point of Contact Recedes Indefinitely

voices

First there was the low voice of a late-night FM deejay and the music. John coltrane maiden voyage miles' brew sarah bessie rainy nights rants and scratchy bluegrass. Sounds beamed down from another star through hot yellow coils that glowed in the dark in my room.

out of the coils

In an isolated fold of the Appalachians, people once sang in place of speaking. Only one song sung by the last remaining man lives on, a tinny field recording.

suspended

I took the blue curtains down, removed the screen, and left the window wide. Would they come for me?

then silent

A man arrived who used words as magic tricks. *I could so easily fall,* he said. *We want what we think we can't have.* He vanished into his black top hat with the tap of a white-tipped wand.

obsessions

Saxophone screams, modal trumpet, sad lady singers, blues shouts, accounts of 19th century explorers, cycle of fifths, maps of countries that no longer exist.

when I was so hungry, when I couldn't sleep

Music thick around me as I danced, a joy slave. The drug the drug the drug—velocity—thumping loud like a fat bass laid down. Under my fan dance. Phone numbers on damp napkins, passport and a plane ticket inside my beaded bag. I never revealed my name.

others, too, pressed on

Some masqueraded as monks. Endured intense weather, hunger, the inability to sleep as they climbed eight thousand meters into the sky. And died or were turned back. Some lost feet to frostbite. Some, fingers.

Voices shimmer high on the Tibetan plateau.

toward the blue peninsula

I toss myself, a loose net, blurring into and out of the sky.

only some are chosen

Whittled to a frayed navy duffel, light on the shoulder, hip bones sharp. I fan a blue book of visas and smudged stamps. A packet of creased maps and chord charts unspools.

back to the blue room

Things left that are no longer. First star. A tall man with a saxophone blows a lullaby of ghosts. I lean into the blue notes. Waves fill the hollow places.

Jo Cannon

Stalker

All summer Jack stalks. Ear to wall, eye to crack, he trails them quietly. By the back door, between hedge and fence, he has made a hide.

His mother says, 'I can't believe it's her. Not that fat cow.'

Jack sees his father flinch. He considers which parent he loves best, or hates least. Like standing on a see-saw, one foot each side of the centre, he can tip either way. He is ten, and soon they will ask him to choose.

'Don't talk to me about fucking chemistry,' his mother says. 'Just don't give me that.'

At night they pour silence like concrete. Afraid they will die, he lies down outside their bedroom door.

His father says, 'After the divorce—'

Sunlight trickles green-yellow through the leaves of Jack's hide. There's a smell of creosote and cat's piss. Jack squirts glue into an empty crisp bag, holds it over his mouth and sucks out the air. He gags as pain punches his temples.

Words thud down a tunnel: *Fat cow. Chemistry. Divorce.*

Elation flares like a firework. He sucks again. His spirits blast upwards. Jack's head and limbs go light and loose and he doesn't care.

He doesn't fucking care.

His parents exchange glances as Jack enters the kitchen. They can't wait for him to leave so they can hurt each other again. His mother fumbles in her bag with trembling fingers.

'Can you nip out for me, Jack? Get us some milk from the shop?'

'Ok, I'll get your fucking milk.'

His words echo far away. Did he say that? Her expression stays the same. His parents are tiny, wingless things that creep round and around, trapped in a jar. She paces, biting her nails. His father leans blank-faced against the wall.

Jack gets as far as the gate and lies down. The earth sweats. Everything is leaking away. A passerby with a dog looks at him curiously. His mother stares from the window and her face alters. He hears the door open. She runs towards him down the path.

Jack thinks, don't even blink.

Carole Burns

The Road Taken

It was her fourth date with her friend's colleague, a doctor, also recently divorced, and she knew, as they drove at midnight from her friend's party, that she was attracted to him, that he was attracted to her, that he was driving them to his home rather than dropping her off at her apartment. She opened her window to the summer night and let her hand flutter in the whoosh of air. She wondered if he would make a pass at her, how a forty-six-year-old once married for nineteen years might make a pass, if by now he'd be an expert, or if he'd forgotten how. Maybe he would kiss her in the car before going in, offer her a drink in the living room, sit close but not too close on the couch, kiss her before clinking glasses, kiss her after, his mouth tasting of red wine. Would he undress her? How quickly might he undress her? She thought about these things and didn't think about these things, wanting to be surprised, as she turned up the volume of the Bach violin sonatas he'd put on, regimented and gorgeous.

From the darkness emerged another night, another drive, with her husband—no, just boyfriend then, not even fiancé yet, so long ago had it become. They were travelling to Cape Cod, listening to a skit on public radio on their way to getting engaged. She wasn't sure that David would propose that weekend two weeks before Christmas, but they had looked at rings together a month or so before, self-consciously, not quite admitting what they were doing, finding out they liked the same style, just a solitaire. She didn't know he had a ring hidden in his luggage somewhere, but then again she did know, and he didn't know she'd say yes and then again he did. And the girl in the skit who had moved to New York from the Midwest like everyone on that program always had, the girl was wondering if she should get married, or if it was too Midwestern. She and David laughed harder at the jokes than they would have on another night, giddy with their secret--they were getting engaged--and with the future beyond that, a wedding, a marriage, children and a house, vacations and jobs and a life that would go on and on like the shadows of scrub trees and sand dunes along Route 6. They didn't know yet that you couldn't predict the future.

She rode with this new man to his house, speeding along the parkway that felt like a country road in Cape Cod more than it felt like Washington, D.C., the sunroof open to the leafy darkness, knowing they would make love that night and then again not knowing, knowing he knew and then again didn't know. The mystery made the night more exciting, it didn't feel set, it didn't feel planned, because they could not know what would happen, not tonight, not ever, and that made her sad as well. Her smallest hope—that they would make love tonight, that it would be lovely—might not come to be. So she released herself to the Bach and the tires spinning pebbles from the road and the way the man she wanted to make love to tapped his fingers in halting halftime to the music, his fingers responding, not his mind, beating the rhythm as the headlights lit the night they were rushing into in quick slices, a few trees, the curving road. Just that.

Shelley McAlister

The Night Swimmers

Reta got the call just as she was getting into bed with a crossword puzzle book. It was nearly eleven and long gone dark. She didn't get to the phone before the answer machine kicked in so she had to press Play. It was a female voice she did not recognise, perhaps a friend of Alison or Nobby. They were night people, always proposing activities much too late. It was Alison who had started the group in the first place, and Nobby who had kept it going all through windy August and drizzly July.

The message was brief: Woodside Beach, half past eleven. A slight pause and then a hint of menace. 'Come on, I dare you.'

Reta put the phone down, shook her head. Of course she wouldn't go, the suggestion was daft. Night swimming was all very well for summer but it was well into October now, autumn. The beach huts would be closed up for the winter, the car park would be desolate. It was eleven o'clock at night and stormy. No one in their right mind would turn up, even on a dare.

A text message came in. Chloe. *'Should we go? What if we don't?'*

Reta hesitated, did not reply. She thought of Alison, who would be at the beach already, swimsuit under her tracksuit, gloating. Nobby would be there too, rubbing his hands together, speculating on who would show up and who wouldn't. Maybe the female message sender would be part of the group. Little old Gert would be there, tough as a walnut, up for it. And the gay guys, Charles and Scott, they would be on their way; they lived just up the hill from Woodside Beach and never missed an opportunity.

Another text message. Chloe again. *'A decision please. SHOULD WE GO?'*

Reta tossed the crossword book onto the bed and started getting dressed. She didn't know why, she had no intention of going. The thought of the icy water and the wind-tossed waves sent a chill through her. She sat on the edge of the bed and put on her shoes, pulled the hood of her sweatshirt up around her ears.

Reta picked up her mobile and texted Chloe: *There is nothing to lose by not going. We should not be bullied into this.*

She put down the phone and fished around in a drawer for her swimsuit.

Chloe rang in tears. 'I don't want to go, I really don't.'

'Me neither,' said Reta, going into the bathroom for a towel. 'I don't think we should go. It's just stupid. I don't even know this person who rang.'

'It'll have something to do with Alison.'

'Or some idea of Nobby's. Some double-double dare.'

'I'm sick of this double dare stuff.'

Reta stuffed a fleece into the bag and shivered. 'Me too. That three o'clock in the morning thing at Monks Bay was the last straw.'

'It wasn't safe. That woman nearly drowned.' Chloe was in tears again, sounded weary. 'I've had a terrible day. It's the last thing I need.'

'But you're going, aren't you?' Reta was surprised at the harshness of her voice.

'Maybe.' Chloe sniffed. 'Probably.' A long pause. 'Yeah.'

Reta slammed down the phone. I have a choice in this, she told herself. I do not have to do it. I am an adult person who can make up my own mind about swimming in a freezing sea on a stormy night in the middle of October. But she was picking up her keys, making for the car.

Luke Thompson

Scarecrow

So we hired this scarecrow. Yincent. My sister saw the ad in the Cambrian News and said 'Is he for real?' so I called him up to see. We met in the afternoon and in the evening I called him again to say the job was his. This was Sunday. I showed him the plot and we watched at the kitchen window so he could see the birds he was meant to scare. He took it all in, but I could see his hands shake. I said 'Are you nervous?' He said he had Essential Tremors and he probably drank too much, but the shaking helped his work. 'Makes you look real,' he said. Before dawn every morning I let the cat out, and I see Yincent setting up. I think it's nice he's there and I wave, and he waves.

Liz Brennan

The frown lines, sagging cheek and neck

fold and trap her inside. Hard times have pursed the lips,
furrowed the brow, and tensed the eyes as if sooner or later water
will seep through. This is the face she's made from her life.
Sometimes it appears as a bright distortion hovering before me as I
drift off to sleep at night, falling into drowsiness and awaiting my
fate like a coin lying in water. I rub it, polish it, until it reflects the
clouds.

Maureen Gallagher

An African Plant Begins with an O

The alert. Coming up to the roundabout. Suddenly—where is she going? Oh Jesus! Where? Where, which exit? WHICH EXIT! City Centre? Clifden? Dublin? Where is she going? City Centre? Clifden? Dublin? THE DENTIST! Third exit. Oh, thank God! Whew!

Crosswords are useful. And she sets herself little tasks now on her daily walk. Like today. Memorising the names of the estates—Rosan Glas, Ceide House, Rosleic. The liquid feel of the words on her tongue. She loves words. And look! That flower again. Idling like an exotic visitor in someone's garden. South African. Quite different from the South African house plant she used grow on her kitchen sill. But that was aons ago. Before she left home to find herself. It was called *African* somethingorother, oh Jesus, African...African....VIOLET! African Violet! Got it!

Now this one. Shape like a daisy. A big fat daisy. A great favourite although it would take over a whole garden if you didn't watch. Pale narrow petals. What's this it's called? A name you could chew. Mesembryanthemum? No! It's something beginning with O. God, she thought she had it for a minute there. Mesembryanthemum: a daisy too and South African. At least she had the genus right. Close. But not there. Osymanthus? Something like osymanthus.

Nearly home.
Osy...osy...oste......oste...ostesper.....OSTEOSPERSUM! THAT'S IT! Ten out of ten! Osteospersum! What a gift! Osteospersum!

Isabel Hicks

Le Roi et ses Bottes

Morning, and the dawn light paints Paris pink. The streets are scattered with pigeons, scavenging the pavements' treasures and gossiping softly. The warm, bitter scent of fresh coffee and bread seep through cafe windows, and the metro below rumbles like the Minotaur treading his labyrinth. The King wakes, and pulls on his boots. His boots are big and green, and his old friends. Every morning, as Paris stirs, the King pulls on his boots and roams the streets of the city. He takes from the bakery's side street the discarded loaves and stale croissants and day-old sandwiches. He gathers the flotsam and jetsam washed up on the market's concrete shores, stuffing celery stalks and small apples into his holdall. He rummages amongst the filth of the *poubelles*, collecting precious edibles; out of date yoghurt, a half-open packet of ham, an unfinished pizza. They are jewels, glittering amongst the surplus. They call him the King because he so proudly walks these streets, surveying his unappreciated kingdom with his boots gleaming green. He has a job, an apartment, and a social security number. He has a master's in Chemistry.

'For ten years,' says the King, 'for ten, fifteen years, I eat nothing but what I find. I haven't fallen sick in ten years. These people, so willing to discard what is so precious, they are the sick ones.'

Rob McClure Smith

Girl, Iowa

It's cold out, night dark as a black diamond, one chalk star clicking on and off. Walking, we don't talk much, any. Boot-soles scuffing the sidewalk and blowback clouds of chill breath company enough. Time was, we did. Time was, his lips unzipped my pants quicker than his fingers, his voice the ring of cool pennies, jingling sugar. He is not really my friend, but I have friends for that. What he is: strong-jawed and with an inclination to incline his hips between my own. I crave his warm mouth still.

Up on the treetops dark crows rustling huddled on the higher branches like dishevelled umbrellas, a kingdom of black-feathered dreams. (Also, on this quiet street, they are very spooky.) He points at a gibbous moon full like a lantern, sky flooding the trees, dots of crows skidding cornfields, same old same old.

I say yes. I've a honeyed tongue and a mouthful of bees.

In the bar there's nobody with teeth. We're skimming the froth of our Guinness when they come in. Unmemorable men as men go. One is thickset and solemn. The other is thin and solemn. I go to the bathroom where it's quiet, listen to my pulse, the milk pushing soft in my veins. I make a study of the yellow brackish backup on the floor tiles and wonder what Iowa means in the native language. The brown paper from the towel rack is coarse against my brow below which eyelashes smudge black strips. I think of oval chocolate Easter eggs with yellow-white cream insides, for no special reason.

I don't know what was said, but the men are hitting him now. He is swinging at them, crying like a fox strangling in an electric fence. The regulars are disinterested, except the waitress, who is enamoured of all this hitting, sizing up the bigger of the two solemn men, imagining how much pummelling a body might enjoy.

One three-day bender ended in a concussion at the tiny zoo in the Quad Cities. That wasted, he becomes docile and enjoys looking at chimps. He is a sentimental soul, my love. That wasted, he may also stagger and flip and crash into a baby stroller and bloody his head and break up with me, only to come crawling back in time into my powder-white sheets, my power-white thighs, because he loves me more than life itself. He says. The summer of the bee-sting that was. August of blowsy ticking thistles and loosestrife, jumbles of Queen Anne's lace.

I thrum my fingers on the smooth wood of the bar till it is over, see shiny bottles all in shiny rows. He thinks his nose is broken, cotton wadding stuffed in a nostril. His abusers buy him tequila and salted peanuts. They contract grain in Salina and are re-evaluating the Burlington-Santa Fe, corn-fed Kansas Republican boys, good company.

Outside comes morning, a broken girl limping out of a frost-blasted orchard. Across stubble fields a shotgun of crows scatter into the pale yellow light. He needs to sit down, back braced against the window of First Glass Inc. He says he loves me as I dab his mouth with my sleeve, wipe the blood-crust half-moon gash beneath his eye. Me, a good corner-man with no towel to throw. He says he is sorry. That tomorrow is another day. It is, again.

If I could, I'd slough off my skin like the years, get a pedicure, a degree that mattered, a Toyota Tercel, a one-way Zephyr ticket out of here.

For now I will keep things like this.

Ben Parker

Lay-by

As so often happens during the early evenings of spring, when he's convinced himself that winter has come to an end, and day will conclude not with a decisive full-stop but with a soothing ellipsis, night occurs instead in a lost moment between the first hint on the horizon and the sudden realisation that it has staked its claim on the whole sky. At these times he feels cheated, as though despite all his best efforts to watch the hand that holds the cards his attention has been artfully diverted just at the point the trick occurs. And on this particular night his disappointment coincides with a stutter from his car's engine, followed by a series of violent jerks as though it were going to stall, before it finally trails off like the end of a bad conversation.

He guides the car from the left-hand lane of the empty dual carriage-way onto the rough ground of the hard-shoulder and comes to an ungraceful stop. For ten minutes he sits. Neither swearing nor moving, nor even angry. Instead he simply cannot believe it has happened to him. Every journey he has taken since he became a driver has included a quick glance out of the passenger window to wonder at the misfortune of the occupants of a hazard-lit vehicle. There is one on every journey. Usually the car doesn't even look old, always the break-down service are yet to arrive. And now, of course, with him the only occupant of this stretch of road, it is finally his turn.

The engine tuts as it cools. He stares ahead, attempting to locate the protocol for this situation, but nothing comes. He is loath to interrupt even the conversation of friends uninvited. The thought of forcing himself without introduction into the evening of a repair service, possibly announced by the simple ring-tone of mobile, but possibly an alarm accompanied by the flashing of an orange light, startling a man from his slumber at the wheel as he dreams of a quiet night with no calls. But he has no torch to check the engine himself, or expertise were he able to see it. There is a blanket on the back-seat and half a sandwich in the glove-box. He resolves to wait. An hour without use might be enough for the fault to abate, and if it is not he will sleep.

Dawn comes and he wakes. A lorry passes. He considers turning the key in the ignition, but decides he is still too tired to drive. He pulls the blanket closer round him and drifts off. Midday and the dual-carriage way rumbles with traffic, he turns his hazards on and sits up, watching the turned faces of drivers as they speed by. He realises he cannot now phone anyone. His engine will be cold and he will have no answer for the inevitable question. How long will his hazard-lights continue to flash? Days? Weeks, probably, if he doesn't use the radio. His account is in credit and he is walking distance from a service station. If he conserves energy there's no reason he can't stay here indefinitely. Tonight he will push the car further from the road, nudge it against the embankment and let grass grow to cover it. Would he report that sight if he passed it? Unlikely, very unlikely.

Ruth O'Callaghan

No Such Place Exists

No such place exists now but the few remaining who can remember its location seek only to forget. They do not speak of the long afternoons when a laze of bees filled the air, when the drip of honey was on every tongue and each man knew the promise.

Neither do they speak of how hurrying villagers crowded the paths which climbed beyond the tree line, determined to seek a place before the sun set and night barred further movement. Friend by friend, neighbour by neighbour, each unaware of the other, they scrambled over dead roots, evaded the grasp of trees and slid face down over scree—no skin was broken. Finally they lay, acquiescent, as the bees, having herded them to this place where the sky began, sang to them in the darkness.

The knowledge given has not been passed onto the children. If they are fortunate they will never know it.

Alice Willingtron

Stretched Voltage

Between the lines of pines and pylons, teenaged years spent hairy-legged in wool socks and boots, the heather impeding. Behind the others, out of breath, catching up only when we stopped. A blister purple under white skin, each step pressing down on the pain. Looking up towards the deer, rain, sunlight, rain.

Finding the pool, the water bounding and subsiding into granite, the sun suddenly staying, and all except me, stripping and plunging, my rucksack digging into my shoulders. One girl getting out, pulling off her tee-shirt and knickers to get dry and me turning away, silent, screwed.

Finishing, everything lighter. The waterfall stays for decades, stretched voltage. Walking up into the pine and crashing of the burn, the sika deer watches with its molten eyes like a young man in the trees, until I smile, and it's gone.

Contributors

Jenny Adamthwaite was born in York in 1982. She now lives in East London where she works as a teaching assistant. She writes poetry and fiction, and her new website can be found at www.jadamthwaite.co.uk. She is currently working on a novel.

Rowyda Amin won the *Wasafiri* New Writing Prize for poetry in 2009 and has had poems published in magazines including *Magma*, *Wasafiri*, *Rising* and *Notes from the Underground*. Her pamphlet in the Pilot series is due to be published in 2010 and her poems will appear in the anthology *Ten* (Bloodaxe, 2010)

Gail Ashton's debut poetry collection is *Ghost Songs* (Cinnamon Press, 2007). She is the co-editor of two poetry anthologies for Cinnamon, *Only Connect* (2007) and *In The Telling* (2009), as well as the author of biographies on Chaucer and Hardy, both forthcoming with Hesperus Press. Her next collection is *Fattening the Albatross* (Cinnamon, 2012).

Brian C. Baer lives in Spokane, Washington in the United States. His absurdly short stories have been published in *The Northville Review* and *365 Tomorrows*, and been produced on The Drabblecast. His blog can be found at BrianCBaer.blogspot.com.

Tina Barry's short stories have appeared in literary magazines, newspapers and trade publications. She is an M.F.A. candidate in creative writing at Long Island University in Brooklyn, New York, where she lives with her husband, the sculptor Bob Barry. She can be reached at tbarrywrites@yahoo.com.

Valerie Bird completed an MA in Creative Writing with Distinction from Southampton University. She has had short stories published in *The New Writer* and in *Staple Magazine*; poems commissioned for two anthologies by Michael and Peter Benton and two poems chosen for anthologies by United Press. She is working on a novel which explores the impact of a covert relationship on the lives of those involved. Two novels are with her agent.

Liz Brennan lives in Sonoma County, CA. Her stories have appeared in a variety of journals including *The Prose Poem: An International Journal, Key Satch(el), Lift, Paragraph,* and *Texture.* She is author of the chapbook *Sewing Her Hand to the Face of the Fleeting* (Quale Press).

Fern Bryant was born in Los Angeles but has lived in London since 1983. She is an academic editor specializing in anthropology, archaeology, and radical philosophy. Enthralled by life on the margins, she is especially fond of wild parakeets, urban foxes and feral terrapins: in short, anything with the potential to cause trouble.

Lisa K. Buchanan started with a journalism degree and a goal of becoming an editor on a women's magazine--once realized, lasting nine months. She has since earned an MFA and published award-winning fiction and essays in commercial (*Redbook, Cosmopolitan*) and literary magazines (*Fourth Genre, Mid-American Review,* and *The Missouri Review*). www.lisakbuchanan.com

Carole Burns is editor of *Off the Page: Writers Talk About Beginnings, Endings, and Everything in Between* (Norton 2008) and runs the MA in Creative and Critical Writing at the University of Winchester. She is at work on a novel, and lives in Cardiff.

Jo Cannon is a Sheffield G.P. Her stories have appeared in *The Reader, Myslexia, Cadenza, Brand* and *New Writer* among others, and in anthologies including *Route* and *Leaf Books.* Competition successes include firsts in HISSAC and Writers Inc, and runner up in Fish International. Jo's debut short story collection, *Insignificant Gestures* was published by Pewter Rose Press in October 2010.

Rob Carney is the author of two books of poems: *Weather Report* (Somondoco Press, 2006) and *Boasts, Toasts, and Ghosts* (Pinyon Press, 2003). His work has appeared in *Mid-American Review, Quarterly West,* and many other journals, as well as *Flash Fiction Forward* (W.W. Norton, 2006). He lives in Salt Lake City.

Phil Carradice is a poet, novelist and historian. He has written over 30 books, the most recent being the novel *The Black Chair* (the story of Welsh poet Heded Wyn) and *Herbert Williams*, a biography in the University of Wales Writers of Wales series. Phil Carradice is a regular broadcaster on Radio 4 and presents the BBC Wales history programme 'The Past Master'. He regularly runs creative writing classes for both adults and children.

Mark Ellis is a liar.

Rachel Eunson is from Shetland. She works as a marine engineer for the Jubilee Sailing Trust, and is studying English with the Open University. In between times she buys notebooks, and then feels the need to justify this by writing in them. Occasionally this writing migrates to other books, like this one.

Rowan B. Fortune left school at the age of six and dedicated his life to becoming a proficient liar. He studied humanities with the Open University and is completing an MA in Creative Writing from Manchester Metropolitan University. He lives in North Wales where he walks up snow-topped mountains and writes deceptions.

Kate L. Fox has always had an interest in creative writing, particularly poetry. She studied English literature as a first degree and won the university creative writing prize. She recently achieved a merit grade for an MA in creative writing. She is a member of several creative writing groups and within her working career has done some copy-writing.

John Freeman's most recent collection is *A Suite for Summer* (Worple, 2007). A selection of his essays on modern poetry, *The Less Received*, was published by Stride 2000. In 2008 he edited *Black Waves in Cardiff Bay* (Cinnamon), an anthology of writing by Cardiff University Creative Writing M. A. students.

Angela France has had poems published in many of the leading journals, in the UK and abroad. She has an MA in Creative and Critical Writing from the University of Gloucestershire and is studying for a PhD. Her second collection, *Occupation* is available from ragged Raven Press. Angela is features editor of *Iota* and an editor of ezine *The Shit Creek Review*. She also runs a monthly poetry cafe, Buzzwords.

Wendy French lives in London and facilitates writing in healthcare and educational settings. She has two full collections of poetry; the latest *surely you know this,* was published in 2009 by tall-lighthouse press. The title is a fragment from Sappho. Wendy will be judging the Torbay Poetry Competition in 2010.

Maureen Gallagher lives in Galway. Her first collection of poetry entitled *Calling the Tune* was published by WordsontheStreet Press in 2008. Maureen's story 'You shouldn't Have To Kill Your Mother' won the Leyney Writers' Short Story Award 2009. She was also a prizewinner in the Wicklow Writer's Short Story Competition 2008.

Tania Hershman's first collection, *The White Road and Other Stories*, (Salt Modern Fiction, 2008) was commended in the 2009 Orange Award for New Writers. Tania is the founder and editor of The Short Review, (www.theshortreview.com), a site dedicated to reviewing short story collections, and 2010 fiction-writer-in-residence in Bristol University's Science Faculty. Read more at www.taniahershman.com

Sarah Hilary won the Fish Criminally Short Histories Prize in 2008. In 2009, she was shortlisted for the Cheshire Prize and nominated for the Pushcart. A column about the wartime experiences of her mother, who was a child internee of the Japanese, was published in *Foto8 Magazine* and later in the *Bristol Review of Books*. Sarah blogs at http://sarah-crawl-space.blogspot.com/

Rhys Hughes is the author of many books and even more uncollected short stories. His blog can be found at http://rhysaurus.blogspot.com. He enjoys the outdoors life, stargazing and eating raw chillies, but dislikes sarcasm, violins and butter.

Non Prys Ifans lives in North Wales and works as a Speech and Language Therapist. She enjoys writing both in Welsh and English and especially enjoys writing microfiction. One day, she hopes to be brave enough to try writing a novel.

Janet Jennings lives in San Anselmo, California with her husband and twin daughters. For twenty years she owned and ran Sunspire, a natural candy manufacturing company. Her poetry has appeared in *Agni online, Atlanta Review, The Bitter Oleander, Bryant Literary Review, California Quarterly, Connecticut Review, Nimrod,* and *Redivider,* among others.

Tyler Keevil is an award-winning author and filmmaker from Vancouver, Canada. His short fiction has appeared in numerous magazines and anthologies, including *New Welsh Review, Planet, Transmission, Brace,* and *Brittle Star.* His first novel, *Fireball,* will be published this autumn by Parthian. He currently lives in mid-Wales with his wife, Naomi.

Sheila Killian writes short fiction and creative non-fiction, and has published in a range of journals. She is working on a novel in what spare time she can find. She lives and works in the West of Ireland, and thinks a lot about South Africa. She is chair of http://www.sowetoconnection.org

Jenny Kingsley is a short story writer and journalist living in London with her family. Her work has appeared in British and American publications. She studied anthropology at the London School of Economics, government at Georgetown University, and creative and life writing at Goldsmiths College. Jenny was once a politician!

Wendy Klein's poetry has appeared in anthologies and poetry magazines. A retired psychotherapist, her first collection *Cuba in the Blood* came out in 2009, and she is working on a second collection while taking part in the Writing School run by the Poetry Business in Sheffield. Her biggest win to date was 1st prize in the Ware Competition 2009.

K. A. Laity is a medievalist, a columnist for *BitchBuzz*, the global women's lifestyle network, and the author of *Unikirja* (Aino Press 2009), a collection of short stories for which she won a Finlandia Foundation grant and the Eureka Short Story Fellowship, and *Pelzmantel: A Medieval Tale* (Immanion Press 2010). www.kalaity.com

Rosi Lalor is a Spanish Scouser who now lives in Brighton where she recently completed an MA in Creative Writing and Personal Development at the University of Sussex. She writes songs, poetry, prose and drama and works with young people with learning difficulties.

Heather Leach's writing has appeared in a number of publications including *Big Issue*, *City Life Stories*, *Mslexia*, *Times Higher Education Supplement*, and BBC radio. She has edited and contributed to books on writing and reading including *The Road to Somewhere* published by Palgrave Macmillan. She lives in Manchester.

Renyi Lim

Amy Mackelden lives in Newcastle upon Tyne, where she teaches, or tries to. Sometimes she wishes life was more like microfiction—concise, containable, bittersweet and beautiful—instead of the messy, sprawling novel it is. One day, she will live in New York.

Phil Madden lives in Abergavenny, and travels extensively in Europe as a disability consultant. He has exhibited his poster poems in Brussels, and just published a limited edition book of poems and engravings of birds *Wings Take Us* with an award winning engraver, Paul Kershaw.

Shelley McAlister grew up on the west coast of America and came to England in 1977. She writes poetry and short fiction for literary and commercial publications. Her poetry collection, *Sailing Under False Colours*, was published by Arrowhead Press in 2004. She lives on the Isle of Wight.

Rob McClure Smith is an expatriate living in Chicago, Illinois. His short fiction has been published in *Barcelona Review, Warwick Review, Chapman, Gutter, Storyquarterly, Fugue* and many other literary journals. He is a previous winner of the Scotsman Orange Short Story Award.

Jane Monson is a freelance writer and teacher in Cambridge. She teaches Creative Writing courses in Cambridge, Harlow and London and writes web-based biographies of Civil Engineers. Jane was short-listed for an Eric Gregory and commended by the New Writing Partnership. Her debut collection of prose poems, *Speaking Without Tongues* is published by Cinnamon Press.

Lynda Nash has a BA honours in Creative & Professional Writing, her work has been published in various magazines and her poetry collection *Ashes of a Valleys Childhood* (Mulfran Press) was published in 2009. She teaches English and Creative Writing and lives in Trethomas with her husband, sons and two cats. http://lyndanash.webs.com/

Ruth O'Callaghan is a Hawthornden Fellow, competition adjudicator, interviewer, reviewer, editor, mentor, and hosts two poetry venues in London. Translated into five languages, she was awarded an Arts Council grant to visit Mongolia to collaborate with women poets on a book, a C.D. and a website. Both her first two collections have completely sold out. Her new collection *Goater's Alley* (Shoestring) will be published March 2010.

Valerie O'Riordan has an MA in creative writing from the University of Manchester. Links to her fiction can be found online at www.not-exactly-true.blogspot.com. She's currently working on her first novel.

Kachi A. Ozumba is a winner of the Commonwealth Short Story Prize and of the Arts Council England's Decibel Penguin Short Story Prize. His debut novel, *The Shadow of a Smile* (Alma Books), was shortlisted for the 2010 Royal Society of Literature Ondaatje Prize.

Ben Parker was born in 1982 and has had work accepted for publication in a number of magazines including *Iota* and *Staple*. He has appeared in the Cinnamon Press anthologies *In The Telling* and *Storm at Galesburg*.

Clare Potter is a performance poet/writer brought up in Blackwood, South Wales. She graduated from the University of Southern Mississippi with an MA in Afro–Caribbean literature. She then moved to New Orleans, where she was a consultant for the New Orleans Writing Project. On returning to Wales after ten years, Clare won the 2004 John Tripp Award for Spoken Poetry and her collection *spilling histories* was published (Cinnamon, 2006). In the last few years, Clare has been involved in collaborative projects with other writers, musicians, artists.

Angela Readman's poetry collection *strip*, poems about women and the porn industry, is out with Salt publishing. Her poetry has won the biscuit competition and ragged raven. She describes her secret love as short stories and flash fiction. This is the first publication she has sent her prose to in years.

Susan Richardson is a poet, performer and educator based in Cardiff. Her Arctic-inspired collection of poetry, *Creatures of the Intertidal Zone*, is published by Cinnamon Press, while her forthcoming collection, *Where the Air is Rarefied*, a collaboration with visual artist Pat Gregory, will be published by Cinnamon in 2011. Susan is one of the resident poets on BBC Radio 4's *Saturday Live*. www.susanrichardsonwriter.co.uk

Mark Rutter

Catherine Smith has twice been shortlisted for the Forward Prize for Poetry. Her short stories have appeared in numerous magazines and have won prizes in local and national competitions. Her first collection of short stories, *The Biting Point*, will be published in 2010 by Speechbubble Books. She teaches creative writing for Sussex University, Varndean College and the Arvon Foundation.

James P. Smythe was born in London, but has spent most of his adult life living in South Wales. In the parts of his life where he isn't writing novels, he writes computer game scripts. He is the author of two novels: *Hereditation* (Parthian, 2010) and *The Testimony* (Blue Door/Harpercollins, 2012).

Michael Spring was brought up in Surrey, went to University in Belfast and now lives in London where he works in a design and marketing agency. He likes nothing better than being at Fakenham races in December. His goal is to write something as good as *The Crying of Lot 49* (Thomas Pynchon) or *The Emigrants* (WG Sebald), but despairs of making it

Matthew Hedley Stoppard is a Derbyshire-born poet. He lives and operates in and around West Yorkshire. His poems have won competitions and been published in various anthologies. He continues to write verse and short stories about colourful moments hidden by the commonplace, and gives public readings where possible.

Jo Swingler recently graduated from Edinburgh University's Creative Writing MSc with distinction. Her poetry and fiction has appeared in various anthologies and journals including *Flashquake, Aesthetica, Textualities, QWF, The Legendary, Gutter, Stolen Stories* and most recently as part of Edinburgh University Library's Mesostic Interleaved project.

Laura Tansley is 26 and currently lives in Glasgow but grew up in Malvern, Worcestershire and studied in Cardiff. She is clearly drawn to downpours as she consistently picks wet places to live.

Luke Thompson returned to study after spending two years living in a series of barns and sheds and selling vegetables, and is now finishing an MA in nature and place writing with Exeter University. He has had reviews, stories, prose poems and articles published in various magazines.

Collin Tracy received her MFA in fiction and publishing arts from the University of Baltimore in 2006. She designed and self-published *The Dead Boyfriend and Others*, a collection of short fiction, and *The Pugilist*, a book of poems about love and boxing. She can be reached at ms.collintracy@gmail.com

Bill Trüb is a writer from coastal New Jersey and a citizen of the world. His work has appeared in three books: *In the Telling* (2009), *Your Messages* (2008) and *The Review of Contemporary Poetry* (2005). Bill wrote this anthology's title piece, 'Exposure', for his MA portfolio at Cardiff University. He is 28 and recently backpacked around Australia.

Herbert Williams' wide-ranging work takes in poetry, novels, biography and history. His provocative story *The Marionettes* won him the Cinnamon Press Novella Prize in 2008. A Fellow of the Welsh Academy, he lives in Cardiff with his wife Dorothy. Phil Carradice's critical study of his work was recently published in the Writers of Wales series.

Robin Lindsay Wilson was born in South Australia but has lived in Scotland for many years. He is Head of Acting at Queen Margaret University, Edinburgh. In 2005 he was presented with a commendation in the National Poetry Competition. His poetry has appeared consistently in many literary magazines across the country and has won a number of awards and prizes. His first collection *Ready Made Bouquets* was published in 2007 by Cinnamon Press. 'The inner world and the outer set one another alight in Robin Lindsay Wilson's poems.' — *Envoi*.

Alice Willington

Maria Winnett grew up in Loughborough. A physics graduate and lecturer in computing, she lives in London with her husband and son. Her poetry has appeared in *South*, and she is currently working on a collection of short stories.

Sue Wood lives in West Yorkshire. She won the 2008 Cinnamon Press Poetry Award and has also been placed in many other national poetry competitions. Her first collection, *imagine yourself to be water*, is published by Cinnamon Press.